HOME COOKING FROM NANTUCKET

A Good Food and Health Guide

HOME COOKING FROM NANTUCKET

A Good Food and Health Guide

By Nancy Asche Ivas

Founded 1910
THE CHRISTOPHER PUBLISHING HOUSE
HANOVER, MASSACHUSETTS 02339

Photos Courtesy of Terry Pommett

Yoga Photos of Sheri Whelden

Cover Art by Lee A. Papale

Second Printing

PRINTED IN THE UNITED STATES OF AMERICA

DEDICATION

This book is dedicated to my husband Donald, son James and
GOD.

INDEX

SOUPS

BREAKFASTS & SNACKS

MAIN MEALS — SEAFOOD

MAIN MEALS — PORK

MAIN MEALS — CHICKEN

MAIN MEALS — BEEF

MAIN MEALS — VEGETARIAN

SAUCES & DRESSINGS

DESSERTS

INTRODUCTION

Welcome to the world of fresh, glorious food and healthful eating choices! I could not imagine a more invigorating and natural environment than the Grey Lady herself, Nantucket Island, to provide inspiration for this book. People have been drawn to Nantucket for centuries as a healing place for body, mind, and spirit. The island provides fresh air, clean, cool water, sunshine, and native vegetables, as well as an abundant supply of seafood from surrounding waters.

Today, people of the nineties pursue good health, yet they want it quickly for their on-the-go lifestyles. With this in mind, I have made my healthy recipes easy to read and elementary to prepare — you'll find them wonderful, delectable dishes. Simple, clean, and easy foods are by no means "fast food." The recipes and nutritional information included in this book have been designed to help you enjoy eating while reaching and maintaining optimum health. I have included detailed nutritional information regarding the art of "eating healthy."

There is so much we can do for our bodies and always so much more to learn. Remember, eating is truly one of life's gifts and pleasures! We can all learn to choose healthy eating patterns and ultimately enjoy our food without fear of guilt. Here's to your health and well-being. ENJOY!

Yours in health,

Nancy Ivas

AUTHOR'S NOTES

I must emphasize that the recipes are to be played with, changed to your liking, and fun. Never take food too seriously or life for that matter. Enjoy each morsel and minute. The calories on each recipe are an approximate guide for reference. Remember, take what you like and leave the rest.

Special thanks go out to all the wonderful women who contributed to this book through their nurturing foods, as well as all the friends and professionals who supported the book's creation. Especially I am grateful to my mother and father who inspired my destiny with nutrition.

NANTUCKET SPECIALTIES

Daffodil Weekend

This now-traditional Nantucket weekend started years ago when six tons of daffodil bulbs were donated to the community for planting, to bring early color to the Grey Lady after the long winter. Festivities start on Friday, shop owners having decorated their windows based on daffodil themes. There is an antique car parade the next day, and this is followed by the annual Tailgate Picnic out in Siasconset. There is a contest for those who set out the most elegant and unique picnics by (or on) their cars, and nonparticipants look on, admire, and afterwards enjoy their own picnic fare. On Sunday, the Daffodil Flower Show takes place, and prizes are awarded for winning flower arrangements.

Christmas Stroll

The idea of the Stroll was conceived by island residents years ago; now it's the event of the year. Held on the first Saturday of December, Christmas Stroll creates a nostalgic atmosphere of old-time holidays. Main Street has lighted trees decorated by Nantucket schoolchildren. The Chamber Music Choir holds a singalong. A quartet clad in Victorian garments serenades the crowd. A brass group strolls and plays. Shops put on their finest array, and serve warming refreshments. Santa arrives on Main Street amidst great rejoicing and happy hoopla. Residents and guests saunter through a town filled with holiday cheer. It's a great way to end another year on the island.

THE BASICS

Food Substitutions:

One Ingredient For *Or* Instead of Another

For these:	*Use these:*
1 whole egg	3 egg whites or egg substitute
1/4 cup baking powder	1/3 cup phosphate baking powder *or* 2 teaspoons cream of tartar, 1 tablespoon baking soda, and 1 tablespoon cornstarch
1 cup sour milk/buttermilk	1 cup milk mixed with 1 tablespoon vinegar *or* 1 tablespoon lemon juice *or* 1-3/4 teaspoons cream of tartar
1 cup whole milk	1/2 cup evaporated milk and 1/2 cup water, *or* 4 tablespoons dry whole milk plus 1 cup water
1 cup skim milk	1/2 cup evaporated skim milk and 1/2 cup water *or* 4 tablespoons nonfat dry milk with 1 cup water
1 tablespoon flour, for thickening	1 tablespoon cornstarch, potato starch, rice starch, or arrowroot starch *or* 1 tablespoon granulated tapioca
1 cup flour, for baking	1/2 cup whole grain, oat bran, or whole wheat flour plus 1/2 cup flour (or to fill cup)
1 cup solid shortening	3/4 cup vegetable oil
1 teaspoon onion or garlic salt	1 teaspoon onion or garlic powder
3 ounces oil-packed tuna	3 ounces water-packed tuna

For these:	*Use these:*
1 ounce cheddar cheese	1 ounce part-skim Mozzarella
1 ounce cream cheese	1 ounce nonfat cottage cheese
1/2 cup tomato sauce	1/2 cup tomato juice
1 tablespoon mayonnaise	1 tablespoon **Mock Sour Cream** (see p. 140) *or* 1 tablespoon nonfat yogurt
1 tablespoon oil salad dressing	1 tablespoon oil-free salad dressing
1 tablespoon whipped cream	1 tablespoon evaporated skim milk, whipped

Labeling

We can learn a lot from a food label, if we know what to look for. The nutrition information is listed in a standard format as follows.

A Standardized Listing: The sample label that appears below for a box of macaroni and cheese shows the information that will be carried on virtually all packaged food.

Serving Size 1/2 cup (114g)

Servings per container 4

Amount Per Serving

Calories 260	Calories from Fat 120

Total Fat 13 g	20%
Saturated Fat 5g	25%
Cholesterol 30mg	10%
Sodium 660mg	28%
Total Carbohydrate 31g	11%
Sugars 5g	**
Dietary Fiber 0g	0%
Protein 5g	**

For each item, figure shows % of recommended daily consumption for a person eating 2,000 calories a day.

Vitamin A 4% • Vitamin C 2% • Calcium 15% • Iron 4%

% of daily requirement for selected vitamins & minerals

• Percents (%) of a Daily Value are based on a 2,000 calorie diet. Your Daily Values may vary higher or lower depending on your calorie needs.

Nutrient		2,000 calories	2,500 calories
Total Fat	Less than	65g	80g
Sat. Fat	Less than	20g	25g
Cholesterol	Less than	300mg	300mg
Sodium	Less than	2400mg	2400mg
Total Carbohydrate		300g	375g
Fiber		25g	30g

Recommended daily requirement amounts of each item for two average diets.

lg Fat = 9 calories
lg Carbohydrates = 4 calories
lg Protein = 4 calories
SOURCE: Health and Human Services Department, Knight-Ridder Tribune

As you can see, the label states the product's serving size, servings per container or package, calories per serving and calories from fat, protein, carbohydrates, fat, sodium, and potassium. Also, it indicates the U.S. Recommended Daily Allowance (RDA) percentage per portion of protein, vitamin A, vitamin C, calcium, and iron.

Nutrition labels may also list optional information such as grams of polyunsaturated and saturated fat, milligrams of cholesterol, and additional vitamin and mineral content.

The label lists ingredients in descending order by weight. In the label above, unbleached wheat flour is the largest single ingredient, followed by malted barley flour, and so on.

NOTE: The government does not require that chemical additives (used in preserving, coloring, or flavoring) be listed. Hopefully, in the future this will change.

How many of these calories come from fat? Simply multiply the number of grams of fat by 9 to find the amount of fat calories in that food. If more than one-third of the calories come from fat, it is a high-fat food.

Remember 1 gram of fat = 9 calories: carbohydrates and proteins have 4.

EXAMPLE: 260 calories. 5g protein, 31g carbohydrates, 13g fat
    13g fat x 9 = 117 calories
    117/260 = 20% calories come from fat. This is a bit high in fat, but below the 30% so it is fine to eat.

Beware of Ingredients Packaged Under Different Names

SODIUM
baking powder
baking soda
plain/flavored salt
self-rising flour
compounds with
   "sodium" in name

SWEETENERS
dextrin
dextrose
fructose
galactose
glucose
lactose
maltose
mannitol
sorbitol
sucrose

SATURATED FAT
animal fat
beef tallow
butter
cream or sweet cream
cocoa butter
coconut oil
hydrogenated or partially
   hydrogenated shortening
lard
palm or palm-kernel oil
sour cream
whole-milk cheese

Look At Labels Closely

Some products may say "no cholesterol," yet the label shows a high-fat content, which is known to contribute to high cholesterol.

Do You Know What These Terms Mean? SURPRISE

Enriched: Some of the nutrients found in the ingredients of the product were lost or taken out during processing and put back in. EXAMPLE: Flour is enriched with B vitamins.

Fortified: The nutrients not normally found in the product were added during processing to add nutritional value.
EXAMPLE: Orange juice can be fortified with calcium.

Imitation: One food contains all naturally occurring nutrients; the imitation has been created to resemble the first, but may not contain all its nutrients.
EXAMPLE: Fresh eggs and imitation eggs.

Sugar-Free and Sugarless: Guarantees that the product does not contain sucrose (table sugar), but it can contain other sugars, such as honey, corn syrup, etc.

Lite: Makes you think the product is low in calories — but it can also refer to the product's texture, weight, and/or taste.

Natural: This can mean the product is free of artificial additives and/or preservatives, or it can mean that no additional ingredients were added during processing, or both of these.

Dietary Supplement: The product has been formulated to supply more than 50% of the Recommended Daily Allowance of vitamins and minerals.
EXAMPLE: Cereal that supplies 100% of the RDA.

Nutrition on the Fast Track:

#1 RULE: Food in its natural state is BEST! Here are some guidelines for stocking your home with food that is healthy and easy to prepare.

ON THE COUNTER:
* * Keep a basket of fresh fruit handy.
* * Fill a cylinder with bread sticks, rice cakes, and unsalted whole wheat pretzels.

IN THE REFRIGERATOR:
* * Fill a container with fresh vegetables (carrots, cucumbers, radishes, etc.).
* * A cup of no-oil dressing.
* * A cup of no-oil fresh salsa.
* * Freshly grated Parmesan cheese (from deli).
* * Part-skim Mozzarella cheese, grated; and some thinly sliced.
* * Part-skim cheese, thinly sliced.
* * Thinly sliced turkey, lean roast beef, and 95% fat-free ham (most deli meats contain additives — use sparingly).
* * Skim or 1% milk.
* * V8™ or tomato juice.
* * Fruit juice to mix with seltzer.
* * Plain or flavored seltzer water.
* * Non-fat yogurt (in place of mayonnaise and sour cream).
* * Fresh pasta.

IN THE CUPBOARD:
* * Variety-type vinegars (raspberry, tarragon, rice, etc.).
* * Safflower oil, or other highly unsaturated oils.
* * Dried pasta.
* * Rice mixes with 3 grams or less fat.
* * Vegetarian refried beans.
* * Corn chips (low-fat and low-sodium).
* * Canned beans.
* * Canned tuna, clams, crabmeat, shrimp for sandwiches and pasta.
* * Cereal: 2 grams of fiber per ounce, and no more than 5 grams of sugar.
* * Bread: whole-grain varieties, pita, that are low-fat.
* * Cookies: low-fat — gingersnaps, fig bars, vanilla wafers.

IN THE FREEZER:
* * Vegetables and vegetable medleys to use in pasta and stir-fries.
* * Frozen low-fat yogurts, ice milk, juice bars, and fudgesicles.
* * Frozen fruit-juice concentrate for drinking and for sweetening foods.
* * Chicken, fish, crabmeat.
* * Low-fat pizza.

NOTE: In order to make this work for you, you must read labels, and be able to use your imagination to create a wonderful, healthful eating experience.

Measurements

3 teaspoons = 1 tablespoon
4 tablespoons = 1/4 cup
5-1/3 tablespoons = 1/3 cup
8 tablespoons = 1/2 cup
12 tablespoons = 3/4 cup
16 tablespoons = 1 cup
1 cup = 8 ounces = 1/2 pint

2 cups = 16 ounces = 1 pint
4 cups = 32 ounces = 1 quart
8 cups = 64 ounces = 2 quarts = 1/2 gallon
16 cups = 128 ounces = 4 quarts = 1 gallon
1 pound flour = 4 cups
1 pound sugar (granulated) = 2 cups
1 pound shortening or butter = 2 cups

(For liquid and dry measurements use standard measuring spoons and cups. All measurements are level.)

Abbreviations

teaspoon = tsp. or t
tablespoon = Tbsp. or T
cup= c.
ounce = oz.
pint = pt.

quart = qt.
gallon= gal.
pound = lb.
package = pkg.
few grains = f.g.

Oven Temperatures

VERY SLOW OVEN = 250° to 275° F.
SLOW OVEN = 300° to 325° F.
MODERATE OVEN = 350° to 375° F.
HOT OVEN = 400° to 425° F.
VERY HOT OVEN = 450° to 475° F.

Metric System

1 cup = 250 milliliters (ml)
1/4 cup = 62-1/2 ml
1 teaspoon = 5 grams (g)
2 tablespoons = 28.35 g

1 pint = .47 liter (l)
1 quart = .95 l
1 gallon = 3.8 l
1 liter = 2.1 pint

Ounces to grams: multiply ounce figure by 28.3 to get number of grams.
Grams to ounces: multiply gram figure by .0353 to get number of ounces.
Cups to liters: multiply cup figure by .24 to get number of liters.

Valuable Vitamins

Water-Soluble Vitamins
B-Complex

B₁ — Thiamin

Supports the gastrointestinal system, nervous and cardiovascular system. Helps prevent indigestion, anorexia, severe constipation, gastrointestinal problems, deficient hydrochloric acid (stomach acid secretion), diminished alertness and reflex responses, fatigue, damage to myelin sheaths (which cover nerve fibers), and a weak heart muscle. May help prevent depression, numbness in hands/feet, fatigue, impaired growth in children, and shortness of breath.

Found in lean pork, beef, liver, whole and enriched grains (flour, bread, cereals), legumes, blackstrap molasses, brewer's yeast, and wheat germ.

B₂ — Riboflavin

Prevents beriberi, tissue breakdown, and inflammation. (A deficiency can be noted around the oral cavity, relating to a swollen tongue, cracks at the corner of the mouth, and/or cracked lips.) Also helps prevent scaly and greasy skin, and baldness. Helps prevent poor digestion, dermatitis, dizziness, eye problems, and mouth inflammation.

Found in: milk, whole or enriched grains, vegetables, organ meats, and brewer's yeast.

Niacin

Improves circulation, reduces cholesterol levels, supports the nervous system, retains healthy skin, tongue, and digestion.

Found in meat, peanuts, beans, peas, and enriched grains.

B₆ — Pyridoxine

Aids in protein metabolism, helps prevent anemia and tuberculosis, helps to support the central nervous system, may aid in relief of painful fingers, joints, and Parkinson's Disease, muscular weakness/lack of control, arthritis, learning disabilities, anemia, hair loss, and convulsions in infants.

Found in grains, seeds, meats, liver, and kidney. Smaller amounts are found in milk, eggs, and vegetables.

Pantothenic Acid

Vital to the body's overall metabolism. May reduce incidence of duodenal ulcers, infection; and may increase one's life span.

Found in milk, egg yolk, liver, kidney. Fair amounts are found in other meats, cheese, legumes and vegetables, blackstrap molasses, prunes, brown rice, cabbage, cantaloupe, and brewer's yeast.

Biotin

Functions as a co-enzyme, assists in fatty acid and carbohydrate oxidation. Deficiency could result in muscular pain, dry skin, and lack of energy. May help hair growth.

Found in tomatoes, corn, soy, unpolished rice, yeast, egg yolk, liver, sardines, legumes, lentils, whole grains, brewer's yeast.

Folic Acid	Co-enzyme which aids in the transfer of purines, thymine, and hemoglobin. Prevents anemia, sprue (a gastrointestinal disease), and reduces tumor growth. May aid in helping alcohol withdrawal symptoms and in preventing birth defects. May reduce rate at which hair turns gray. Found in green leafy vegetables, asparagus, liver, kidneys, brewer's yeast, root vegetables, tuna, oysters, salmon, and whole grains.
B_{12} — *Cobalamin*	Well-known for boosting energy and preventing pernicious anemia with intramuscular injections. Aids in the treatment of sprue. May help with alcohol withdrawal, cirrhosis of the liver, may reduce cancer growth, osteoporosis and osteoarthritis, decrease mental confusion, and relieve bursitis. May help prevent growth failure in children, brain damage, neuritis, nervousness, speaking difficulties, and poor appetite. Found in liver, fish, dairy, lean meats, and eggs.

Note: No RDA requirements have been set for these water-soluble vitamins.

Choline	Minimizes excess fat deposits, helps transport fat and cholesterol, nerve transmission; aids in gall bladder regulation, lecithin formation, hair growth, and thymus gland. May help prevent cirrhosis, bleeding stomach ulcers, high blood pressure, and growth problems. Found in green leafy vegetables, lecithin, egg yolks, brewer's yeast, fish, legumes, soy beans, wheat germ, and organ meats.
Inositol	Vital for hair growth, metabolizing of fats and cholesterol, formation of lecithin; good for vital organs. May help prevent high cholesterol, skin problems, constipation, and eye problems. Found in citrus fruits, nuts, milk, meat, brewer's yeast, blackstrap molasses, whole grains, vegetables, and lecithin.
Vitamin C (Ascorbic Acid)	Prevents scurvy. Aids in wound healing, fevers and infections, reduces stress, helps proper growth in children. Boosts the immune system. Found in fresh fruits, especially citrus, and vegetables such as tomatoes, cabbage, potatoes, chili peppers, and broccoli.

Fat-Soluble Vitamins

Vitamin A (Retinol)	Aids vision, growth and reproduction function. Increases mucosa membrane flow to carry out infection. Lubricates the eyes, respiratory tract, gastrointestinal tract, genitourinary tract, skin and tooth formation. Found in mainly yellow- and green-colored vegetables and fruit, eggs, dairy products, beef liver, kidney, milk, and fish liver oil.
Vitamin D	Formed in the reaction of skin to sunlight, promotes bone mineralization. Found in yeast, fish liver oil. Milk and margarines are fortified with Vitamin D.

Vitamin E   Helps in protecting the lining of the lungs from air pollution and smoking, reduces benign breast cysts, reduces arterial blockage (which may cause muscle cramps), reduces sickle cell anemia, infant blindness, and aging adrenal glands.

Found mainly in vegetable oils. Also in milk, eggs, muscle meats, fish, cereals, wheat germ, and leafy vegetables.

Vitamin K   Catalyzes the synthesis of blood-clotting factors.

Found in green leafy vegetables, tomatoes, cheese, egg yolk, and liver.

YOUR HEALTH AND NUTRITION

An Important Step In Weight Management: A Food Journal

Why is a food journal (or food diary) so important?

A food journal is a key factor in maintaining your weight or losing weight. A diet program begins with an honest appraisal of your eating habits, so that you can slowly work into a healthy new lifestyle. That means your food journal will record your every meal, snack, munch, gulp, sip, and nibble. Don't skip recording "bad" or "unusual" days. This is not a test. Your food journal will cue you in on habits that need to change in order to keep the weight you have or get it off!

There are many ways to keep a food journal. I find it is easiest to get a spiral notebook and make section columns for each day. Your sections should include *time, place, activity, food, amount of food* and your *emotional state*. Give a full description of each food, including type of preparation (example: "steamed"); any additives (example: "cream in my coffee"); your feelings (example: "tired"); water intake; and amount of exercise.

After three to five days, you can make an appointment to see a good nutritional counselor (check reliable and reputable health or exercise clubs or organizations) so that she or he can make an assessment. Here, you will be able to begin to change old destructive eating habits to new, healthy ones.

Remember: there are no right or wrong answers. Your goal in keeping this food journal is to get an honest, realistic look at your normal eating habits.

And also remember: *Successful weight-losers do not go on diets: they change their way of life*

Wonderful Water

WATER IS THE MOST ESSENTIAL NUTRIENT IN OUR BODY! You should drink at least eight 8-ounce glasses per day. Why?

• Water aids in digestion.
• Water helps to regulate your body temperature.

11

- Water acts as a hunger suppressant.
- Water reduces fluid retention and bloating by flushing out excess sodium.
- Water helps to reduce fat and aids in weight loss by the transportation of fat enzymes.
- Water helps to eliminate waste products.
- Water helps to prevent constipation.
- Water improves glandular function.

As you can see, water means a lot to our bodies. Your body will find its internal balance of water when it is given enough. Remember: sun, saunas, caffeine, alcohol, and exercise deplete your water supply, so replace it. Water content varies from place to place. You may prefer bottled water (not seltzers), adding lemon, lime, orange, or a strawberry to it to cut that heavy mineral taste. Keep water by your side all day. Fill a plastic water bottle with water and keep it and a lemon in your car. Drink a glass of water before you eat a meal. Soon you will see how easy it is to drink two quarts a day.

Eating Out

TERMS YOU SHOULD KNOW
Learn which terms mean low-fat preparation. Order:
- "steamed"
- "in its own juice"
- "garden fresh"
- "roasted"
- "poached"
- "broiled"
- "tomato juice"
- "baked"
- "dry boiled" (in lemon juice or wine)

Some preparations may be low in fat but high in sodium. Watch for:
- "pickled"
- "in cocktail sauce"
- "smoked"
- "in broth"
- "in tomato sauce"

Food descriptions will warn you of high saturated fat preparation:
- "buttered," "in butter sauce"
- "fried," "sautéed," "braised," "pan-fried," "crispy"
- "in cream sauce," "creamed," "in its own gravy," "Hollandaise"
- "in cheese sauce," "escalloped," "au gratin," "Parmesan"
- "stewed," "basted," "marinated" (in oil)
- "casserole," "hash," "pot pie"

Even if you are not trying to lose weight, here are some questions to ask your waiter or waitress to ensure that you'll enjoy a healthier meal:

1. Do you serve margarine instead of butter?
2. Do you serve skim or low-fat milk?
3. Can you prepare my dish using vegetable oil or margarine?
4. Can you prepare my poultry without the skin?
5. Can you make my meat serving a 4-ounce portion?
6. Will you leave all butter, gravies, and sauces off my dish or serve them on the side?
7. Will you serve my salad dressing on the side?
8. Do you prepare dishes without salt or monosodium glutamate (MSG)?
9. Can I call in special requests ahead of time?
10. Do you have a nonsmoking section?

Most important, do not become discouraged. Even if it is an overly busy restaurant and the waiter or waitress seems too busy, make your requests known.

IT'S YOUR LIFE! Enjoy.

GENERAL SURVIVAL TIPS ON EATING OUT

- Avoid fried foods (no matter what).
- Ask to have your food prepared the way you want it. (Be assertive.)
- Read the menu carefully. Ask how items are prepared before you order.
- Select broiled, roasted, baked, poached, or steamed items.
- Start your meal with a green salad, a glass of water, or a clear broth soup.
- Have sauces and salad dressings served on the side.
- Choose restaurants that serve healthy meals — meaning foods served in a natural state. Example: Oriental restaurant as opposed to a fast-food joint. Both can be inexpensive and quick, but the Oriental restaurant can prepare foods in a healthier way.
- Italian restaurants are also a good choice. Choose pasta in a tomato-based sauce. Avoid cream or oil-based foods.
- Oriental restaurants have wonderful vegetable dishes, as well as lots of fish, and they are usually willing to prepare it any way you like.
- If you must go to fast-food restaurants, choose foods lowest in fat — for example, broiled hamburger — and avoid sauces, roast beef, and the salad bar.
- At delicatessens, choose turkey or chicken breast, lean roast beef, and low-fat cheeses; also cole slaw, pickles, and vegetables.
- When dining out with friends, it may get very tempting to throw away diet techniques. Discuss your diet objective out loud; this usually will trigger emotional support from yourself and others. Concentrate on low-fat foods, or if all else fails, excuse yourself from the table for a minute so you can collect yourself and think about what's best to order.
- When flying, call the airline at least 24 hours in advance to request low-fat and low-cholesterol meals.
- Control portion sizes. Eat only the amount of food that is correct for your diet.
- Share dessert with a friend or order fresh fruit or sorbet.

Checking Your Diet:
Resource For Lowering Your Fat Intake

For meat and protein food, CHOOSE:
fish, shellfish, chicken and turkey without skin, ground turkey, lean beef, veal, lamb, pork with very little marbling, dried beans, lentils, split peas, tofu, 2 egg yolks a week.

Limit:
fried, and heavily marbled meats, fatty meat, bacon, sauage, high-fat deli meat, liver, organ meats.

For milk, cheese, and dairy, CHOOSE:
skim or 1% milk only, low-fat or nonfat yogurt, frozen low-fat or nonfat yogurt, low-fat cheeses, 1% cottage cheese, skim milk Ricotta and Mozzarella, evaporated skim milk for coffee in place of cream.

Limit:
whole milk, cream, half & half, ice cream, whole milk, cheese (e.g., cheddar), sour cream, whipped cream.

For bread and cereals, CHOOSE:
plain whole-grain breads, English muffins, bagels, hot or cold cereals with no fat added, low-fat snack foods (e.g., pretzels, popcorn), Norwegian flatbread, rice cakes, Melba toast, low-fat baked goods (e.g., angel food cake, graham crackers, fruit cookies, gingersnaps, fortune cookies, pasta, rice, raisin bread).

Limit:
commercial baked goods (e.g., pies, cakes, doughnuts, croissants, pastries, high-fat cookies, crackers, muffins, biscuits), egg noodles, granola with coconut added, fried rice.

For fruits and vegetables, CHOOSE:
several servings of these low-fat, highly nutritious foods daily — fresh and frozen are best — steamed, boiled, baked, or stir-fried with herbs, lemon and very little unsaturated fat.

Limit:
vegetables prepared in butter, deep-fried vegetables, cream or cheese sauce on vegetables, coconut.

For high-fat foods, CHOOSE:
margarine or diet margarine made with safflower, corn, or sunflower oil, cooking oils such as olive and peanut, or safflower, corn, sunflower, soybean oil, salad dressings made without saturated oils, nut snacks in moderation (can be high in calories and high in total fat even though it is primarily unsaturated).

Limit:
butter, margarine made with partially hydrogenated oil, lard, meat fat, hydrogenated or partially hydrogenated vegetable shortening, coconut oil, palm or palm kernel oil, salad dressings made with sour cream, cheese, egg, or mayonnaise, chocolate.

Affirmations

We are creatures of habit, and as we become more aware, we see repetitive patterns that can cause distress in our lives (such as worrying or projecting). Awareness is the start to breaking these negative thoughts or behaviors, but it is the implementing of positive ones that creates a peaceful and healthier lifestyle.

Affirmations can increase positive awareness and program your body and mind into a focus of well-being. It works like this: Choose a short phrase with special meaning to you and use it as often as you can throughout the course of the day. Keep working with these positive mediations and see how effective they can be!

Some Examples:
(Breathing is very important.)

- *Everything I eat enhances my healthy body.*
- *I love you, (your name). (Try this looking in the mirror.)*
- *I meet life with happiness and joy.*
- *All is well.*
- *Not my will, but thine be done.*
- *It is safe for me to feel good.*
- *I am relaxed and happy.*
- *I am positive about my life.*
- *Easy does it.*
- *Keep it simple.*

New Habits For Life

MAKE NEW HABITS — ONES YOU CAN LIVE WITH! GRADUALLY MAKE CHANGES IN YOUR MEALS, EXERCISE REGIME, AND BUYING PATTERNS. WE HUMAN BEINGS TEND TO OVERINDULGE IN ALL AREAS. WE GET EXCITED ABOUT OUR NEW DIET, OUR NEW EXERCISE, OUR NEW LOOK, BUT AFTER A FEW WEEKS OR MONTHS, WE'RE BACK TO OUR "OLD WAYS." PREVENTION IS OUR BEST CURE. TAKE THINGS SLOWLY, KEEP IT VERY SIMPLE, AND WORK TOWARD YOUR GOAL ONE DAY AT A TIME.

Tips To Help You Maintain Your Ideal Weight

1. FIRST and foremost in any diet regime is to keep an accurate food journal. In this, include: time, place, activity, food, amount of food, and your emotional state. (See page 11, "An Important Step in Weight Management: A Food Journal.")
2. Get at least 20 to 60 minutes of brisk (aerobic) exercise three to five times a week. Try power walking, jogging, biking...or try something new for the new you!
3. To make food portions look larger, use smaller plates.
4. Avoid mindless munching. Pay attention to what your body consumes. Don't get lost in your favorite soap opera or book; don't eat while holding conversations on the telephone.
5. Plan your grocery list well, and shop just after you have eaten. This will reduce impulse purchases. STICK TO THE LIST! (See page 18, "Supermarket Checklist.")
6. Eat more slowly, and enjoy each morsel. Eat food as you cut it, rather than all at once. And don't forget — *chew, chew, chew* your food; give your digestive tract a break. Even count the number of times you actually chew each bite, and set your utensils down after each bite.
7. Fill up on the bulk of whole fruits, fresh vegetables, and whole grains. These carbohydrates satisfy the appetite and add fuel to energize you.
8. Never go to a party famished. Have a glass of carbonated water with a piece of fruit before you leave home. If that is impossible, have a glass of seltzer at the function, before you head to the buffet table or order from the menu.
9. Monitor your consumption of alcohol; it packs a significant number of calories, and when ingested is utilized as caloric fat in your body.
10. Brush your teeth, use mint spray, or chew sugarless gum while preparing dinner and clearing the table. You will be less likely to pick.
11. Eat only three meals a day, at specified times and places. Set your table as formally as possible, with complete silverware service. Make mealtime special and a specific part of your daily routine.
12. If your motivation starts to fade, LIFT the amount of weight you've lost — a 5-pound hand weight — and work out or, as weight gets heavier, lift a 20-pound frozen turkey. This will give you an image of how far you have come and what a lot you've accomplished.
13. LEARN to distinguish between "stomach" hunger (stomach growling) and "mouth" hunger (the oral fixation that made us overweight to begin with)! This knowledge will redeem you from eating that pint of Heavenly Hash ice cream and propel you instead to indulge in a slushy glass of natural sherbet.
14. Do not let emotions set you back. When you're depressed, bored, frustrated, nervous, angry, lonely, tired, or still very hungry, call a friend; call a counselor; go to a meeting for overeaters. Learn to vent these feelings toward a positive and creative NEWyou!
15. Don't let the people around you affect your new behavior. If they are eating or drinking and you are not hungry, nurse a glass of seltzer water with a slice of lemon, lime, or orange in it.
16. Bring healthy snacks (e.g., apples) with you, so that you are ready to energize yourself with nourishing food, if your day gets too busy for a sit-down lunch.
17. Be aware that caffeine stimulates your appetite. Try to limit caffeine intake.

18. Practice portion control. Don't serve meals family-style (all the foods set out on the table at once). Portion food onto plate by the stove. IF YOU MUST HAVE THAT FOOD, let your passion be in moderation. REMEMBER: It is the practice of these principles that will keep you healthy!

19. Try to consume most of your calories early in the day. This gives your body time to work it off again. Eat like a king at breakfast, a prince at lunch, and a pauper at dinner. Don't eat after 6:30 p.m., if possible.

20. Don't buy high-calorie snacks. This is where your new adjustments will go into practice. Prepare low-calorie snacks and keep them on hand. Keep a list of "good" snacks and have it nearby, until you find what you like and incorporate it into your memory.

21. Let your friends, family, and colleagues know that you are in pursuit of a healthful existence for yourself. They will appreciate you sharing your goals, and may ask you how they, too, can become fit!

22. You have to or want to lose weight and become healthy because YOU ARE A WONDERFUL PERSON, not because you want to become one.

23. Reward yourself as you attain your goals, or have kept the weight off for a certain amount of time. For example, buy a new book, get a facial, put a certain amount of money away for a vacation or new sporting equipment.

24. Keep busy, and you will not find time to fill up with food.

25. Have a bowl of soup or a glass of water before you eat dinner. This will take the edge off and keep you from "ravenous eating."

26. IF YOU SLIP, do not burden yourself with guilt. Make a note in your food diary and make necessary changes so it will not happen again, or as often.

27. If you must, MUST buy junk food, purchase it in single-serving packets. It may cost more, but it will keep you from losing control.

28. Do not skip meals. This habit tricks you into thinking you "deserve" to eat more. Again, eat only three meals a day.

29. Rely on aerobic exercise to burn off fat, build a strong body, and increase your cardiovascular endurance. This also will help keep your body running efficiently and bring your weight set point to a desired level.

    Weight set point: The point at which your body functions at a certain weight. By bringing this set point lower or higher, your body learns to function at its new weight.

30. Never allow yourself to gain over 5 pounds of your ideal weight. This is RED LIGHT time. The alarm is on! So decide on a reasonable weight range, rather than one number (e.g., 130-135).

31. Take just a taste of the food you crave so badly, then tell yourself it will all just be the same. Or better yet, walk yourself through eating a whole piece of pie or a whole sundae. Think of your emotions before you eat: How do you feel? How do you feel while you are eating it? Finally, how do you feel when you have finished it ALL? Write your reactions in your food diary.

32. There is no secret to staying happy and healthy. It takes a conscious effort on your part, but you will also reap the *grand reward!* Fill half your stomach with food, one-fourth with water, and one-fourth with positive and happy thoughts.

33. Learn to alter your recipes to fit your new lifestyle. Keep a list on hand for quick reference — e.g., mustard instead of mayonnaise or butter, nonfat milk for whole milk.

34. Measure your success by how you FEEL, and how your clothes fit. NOT by what the scale says.

35. *Deal with one meal at a time!* Make sure what you put into your body is healthful. If you take each meal as it comes along, you will see the weeks and months take care of themselves.

36. Learn to eat when you are hungry and STOP when your hunger has been satisfied. A lot of extra food is eaten because you are tired (right after you get home from work), so identify your feelings.

37. Cultivate ACTIVITY AWARENESS within yourself. Plan activities daily for yourself. When you get home from work, walk the dog, open the mail, take a shower.

38. Never buy clothes TOO BIG; this will give you an excuse to grow into them!

39. Make rules for yourself; be creative and have fun with being fit. Learn all you can about nutrition, send for newsletters, attend seminars. Be excited about being alive, and that you have the power to enjoy every single minute of it!

40. Remember that fat is stored, muscle tone is not. Exercise is vital for your health. Walk or bike whenever you can instead of driving. Get off the bus before your stop and walk the rest of the way. Park the car farthest from your destination and walk the rest of the way. Answer the farthest phone in the house. Take the stairs when you can.

41. Please remember: This is a new way of life for you. Keep things simple! Nourish yourself physically, emotionally, and spiritually. Give the good news of living a healthier life to your loved ones.

Supermarket Checklist

Life's basic physical necessities are food, clothing, shelter, love, and utilities. The food you can forego on your next trip to the market is totally up to you. However, it helps to think carefully about what foods are really necessary, as well as economically prudent, in a healthy diet.

Here are a few helpful tips:

BEFORE GOING TO MARKET
- Check your supplies. Open your cabinets, refrigerator, and freezer and see what is on hand, and use what you have in future meals. Try to keep major shopping to two times per month. The fewer trips to the store, the more money saved.
- Know your prices. Be aware of the "regular" prices of items. Items marked on sale or in bargain boxes may not be on sale at all! It pays to take the time to comparison-shop before and while you are at the market.
- Check coupons. Be selective. Use the coupons for items you normally buy anyway. Usually a few cents off is no bargain; neither is an item that your family won't eat anyway.
- Know your market or markets. Memorize the layout of each market and use it as you make out a shopping list. This will help you to save time and avoid temptation of foods you don't need.
- Make a shopping list. Put down items you know you need and can use. List the items according to the path you mentally make out in your mind. Try not to backtrack down any aisle. Check off items as you go along.

- Eat first. Never go to the market hungry! If you are hungry while shopping, you increase the risk of impulse shopping. Remember, stick to the list!
- Choose your shopping companions carefully. Shop by yourself whenever possible. Try to leave the children at home. If this is impossible, let them help to get the items on the list and also to prepare for shopping at home. Even toddlers can help by opening cabinets at home for inventory. Teenagers can clip coupons. Remind children that thrifty shopping can lead to money saved toward the purchase of other items. And children are not the only ones who can throw you off. Watch out for impulsive shopping by spouses and other adults.

AT THE MARKET:
- Don't rush. If you rush, chances are you won't take the time to comparison-shop and check labels for nutrient and fat content, or to determine whether the family-size or generic brand actually saves you money.
- Buy produce and meat first. These items account for the largest portion of your budget. You might be better off purchasing meal alternatives such as beans or peanut butter.
- Watch for unadvertised specials. Sometimes these will be displayed on carts and in certain sections of the store. Make sure you compare these items with household needs. Do you really need a 100-pound bag of potatoes for two people?
- Buy store or generic brands. Unless a specific brand makes the difference, take advantage of the generic and store brands. Often they are the same product in different wrapping.
- Think of the environment. The fancier the package, the more it is overwrapped, the higher the cost economically and environmentally. Put cleaning, paper, and miscellaneous products last on your list. You can save up to 75% of the cost of cleaning products if you think natural. And please choose products that are environmentally safe. For example, use cleaning and dusting cloths made from old rags; use baking soda for cleaning countertops and sinks; use ammonia for windows and floors.

Most of all in your supermarket shopping, be aware — you may end up with a thicker wallet!

SPICE AND HERB CHART

Below is a list of herbs and spices most commonly used in the home, along with their healing qualities.

Name/Part Used	Therapeutics/Conditions
Aloe/juice & gel	Rejuvenating, laxative, intestinal cleanser — used for liver dysfunction, menstrual disorders, cuts, wounds, burns (especially sunburn), menopause, constipation, obesity, regulation of bowel movements, acne, boils, skin rashes, bursitis, worms, and hemorrhoids.
Basil/leaves	Stimulant — used for mental dullness, depression, colds, cough, sinus, nausea, congestion, headaches, arthritis, fever, intestinal gas or indigestion, nervous conditions, used topically as an insect repellent, kidney/bladder problems, constipation.
Bay/leaves	Stimulant — tones and strengthens digestive organs; cramps, prevents gas and indigestion.
Black pepper/dried peppercorns	Stimulant — expectorant, increases gastric secretions, good for lack of appetite, indigestion, obesity, flatulence, cold extremities, colds/sore throats, excess mucus; strengthens heart; antifungal/antiparasitic properties.
Cayenne/powder pods	A heart and circulatory stimulant — good for sore throat, cold extremities, indigestion; clears toxins in the colon; useful with weak immune system, lack of energy; normalizes blood pressure; good for candida, worms, muscle pain, arthritis, neuralgia; helps with adverse reactions to alcohol; helps prevent heart attacks/stroke.
Camomile/tea	Relaxant — stomach ache, headache, nervous digestion, colic, hysteria, abdominal cramps, difficult menstruation, eye inflammation; calms nerves; helps prevent nightmares, diarrhea; rinse for hair. Oil used for baths and aromatherapy.
Cinnamon/bark as a powder	Stimulant — used for colds, cough, bronchitis, asthma, laryngitis, low back pain, hiccups, toothache, nerve pain, weak digestion, diarrhea, heart and abdominal pain, menstrual cramps; may help to balance insulin levels.
Comfrey/root & leaves	Fractures, bruises, burns, sprains, asthma, ulcers, boils, blood in urine, respiratory and digestive disorders, lungs, cough, kidney and bladder ailments, hemorrhoids, general debility; also infection fighter, blood cleanser.

Coriander/leaves & dried seeds	Stimulant — diuretic, burning urination, cystitis, urinary-tract infection, skin rashes, measles, hay fever, indigestion, hyperacidity, flatulence; good for appetite, relieves diarrhea, strengthens the heart, increases gastric juices.
Caraway seeds	Aids in digestion, reduces flatulence, improves appetite, good for colic and nervous conditions.
Fennel/root & seeds	Stimulant, diuretic, antispasmodic — good for weak/nervous digestion, nausea, vomiting, abdominal pain, gas or cramping, difficult/burning urination, colic in babies and children, heartburn, eyewash, gout, spasms; promotes breast milk; liver cleanser, expels mucus.
Garlic/cloves & bulb	For colds, cough, digestion, arteriosclerosis, indigestion, hysteria, lung conditions, arthritis, sciatica, low resistance, abdominal pain/cramping, cancer, toothache, earache; lowers high blood pressure, raises low blood pressure; decreases blood cholesterol, blood sugar, blood clotting, impotence; strengthens nerves; kills parasites and infections.
Ginger/root	Stimulant — expectorant for lungs, good for circulatory system, sore throat, colds, flu, bronchitis, asthma, headache, laryngitis, arthritis, indigestion, vomiting, colic, delayed menstruation, muscle ache, heart weakness, nausea, poor circulation, flatulence, travel/motion sickness, morning sickness, cold extremities, pneumonia; cleanses kidneys/bowels; helps nutrient absorption; detoxifies system; helps hair growth when massaged into scalp; strengthens stomach and digestive tract.
Licorice/root	Laxative; also used for sore throat, cough, laryngitis, bronchitis, ulcers, hyperacidity, burns, abdominal pain, painful urination, general debility, hypoglycemia, heartburn, colic; strengthens heart and circulatory system; promotes breast milk; stimulates kidney and bowel function; anti-inflammatory, anti-arthritis, antibacterial; reduces fever; neutralizes toxins; lowers blood cholesterol.
Nutmeg/seed	Prevents gas/fermentation in stomach, vomiting, nausea, diarrhea, abdominal pain and distention; also used for insomnia, nervous disorders, impotence, indigestion.

Parsley/leaves, roots, & seeds	Used for urinary-tract infections, gout, as diuretic; also for edema, swollen glands, swollen breasts, delayed or painful menstruation, kidney stones, gallstones, low back pain, liver ailments; promotes breast milk; tones uterine muscles; strengthens digestion; supports blood vessels, capillaries, and arteries.
Peppermint/leaves	For colds, flu, fever, sore throat, nausea; vomiting, indigestion, depression, headaches, hysterics, sinus, muscle spasms/cramps, ringworm, colic, flatulence, ulcers; antiparasitic; anti-inflammatory; stomach relaxant; stimulates liver and gallbladder.
Saffron/stigmas/styles in powder form	For menopause, menstrual pain/irregularity, sexual debility, infertility, anemia, liver weakness, hysteria, depression, neuralgia, low back problems, diarrhea, indigestion, asthma, palpitations, gout, arthritis, colds.
Sage/leaves	For cold, flu, cough, sore throat, laryngitis, swollen lymphatics, night sweats, spermatorrhea, hair loss, nervousness, mental exhaustion, hot flushes, painful menstruation, infected gums, mouth ulcers, amenorrhea, sinus congestion; stops lactation.
Turmeric/root	Used for shoulder pain, menstrual cramps/irregularity, colic, poor circulation, anemia, obesity, diabetes, acne, bruises and wounds; improves liver function; breaks up congestion; detoxifies food; reduces fevers; purifies blood; has antifungal properties; heals wounds internally and externally.
Thyme/flower	Good for sore throat, colds, cough, worms, indigestion, infected gums, bronchitis, larnyngitis, whooping cough, flatulence, rheumatic pain, infection, migraines, bad breath, colic; antibacterial, antifungal; kills intestinal worms; removes excess mucus from the head, lungs, and respiratory passages; helpful for lack of appetite.

Although there are many other beneficial herbs, I have only listed the ones common in everyday cooking. None of the herbs and spices are intended to be used as a substitute for medical treatment; this listing is for information only.

SEASONAL HEALTH

Each season brings about change in nature and in our bodies. Our bodies have specific reactions to these cycles. This can be a stressful time (each change in season), so prevention and staying healthy should be our primary goals.

Here is a basic guide for keeping balanced throughout the seasons. It is important to prepare and listen to internal cues carefully. Learn what a pleasure it is to take control of your own health.

SPRING
Characteristics: Color: Green
Element: Wood for growth and restoration
Yoga posture associated with Spring: Trikonasana (Triangle)

Nutrition: Clearing the body of old patterns is a natural way of spring cleaning; physically, mentally, emotionally and spiritually. It is a perfect time of the year to do a simple fast by drinking nourishing liquids and/or eating fresh fruits and vegetables. This can be done for one or up to several days. One must eat or drink every two hours to keep the blood sugar from dropping too low and to sustain energy. Another type of cleanse is the Elimination protocol.

Each day you eliminate a specific type of food until you are eating only fruits and vegetables. Then each food group gets added in one day at a time.

Day 1 — Eat normally. Note patterns of when, what and how much you eat.

Day 2 — Eliminate processed, preserved or chemical derived foods.

Day 3 — Eliminate Meat.

Day 4 — Eliminate Dairy.

Day 5 — Eliminate Grains, Breads and Starches.

Day 6 — Eat only fruits and vegetables. Also, drink plenty of water.
*Watch that blood sugar levels stay stable, so eat or drink every two hours.

Day 7 — Add Grains, Breads and Starches.

Day 8 — Add Dairy.

Day 9 — Add Meat.

Day 10 — Add processed, preservatives or chemicals, only if necessary.

Day 11 — Eat normally.

In summary: Any food or food group that makes you feel sluggish, gives you a headache, or plain makes you feel bad...ELIMINATE IT! Generally, those foods which cause cravings could mean there is an allergy present so beware.

Relaxing, breathing and chewing well enhance food absorption and aids digestion. The liver and gallbladder are easily stressed during this season. Eat foods that work harmoniously with these organs, for they will keep the body functions working efficiently. These foods include: All fruits (except avocados), all grains, all vegetables and especially beans, low-fat yogurt and cottage cheese, potatoes, turkey, fish, shellfish, pasta, and popcorn. Low fat and high fiber foods are preferred.

CHECK YOUR BALANCE

Balanced: Focus on new beginnings, spring cleaning of environment and body. Exercise on a consistent basis, do some gardening, feel enthusiastic and creative. Let go of old stuff:

Out of Balance: There will be excess in all forms — drugs, sweets, alcohol. Overeating and laziness will overcome you. There will be the same old things clogging your life and internally you may become constipated or congested.

SUMMER

Characteristics: Color: Red   Element: Fire for energy and circulation
Yoga posture associated with summer: Janu sirsasana

Nutrition: Balancing your diet along with proper exercise is important during the summertime. The reason for this is that certain organs need extra care now. They are the heart and small intestine. Both benefit greatly from adequate amounts of exercise and fresh foods. The body will experience higher levels of energy and achieve potentials when damaging foods are removed from the diet. These harmful foods include: Processed foods, foods with chemical or preservatives added, alcohol, coffee, tea, tobacco and any food that causes allergic reactions. Reducing the intake of high fat meats, dairy and other "heavy" type foods helps too. Summer is the time to take charge and recharge...

CHECK YOUR BALANCE

Balanced: Enjoying sunshine, having fun, laughing, exercise, increased vigor, and eating lighter.

Out of balance: Feeling fearful, overeating (especially overeating those damaging foods listed above), being too serious, faint at heart.

LATE SUMMER

Characteristics: Color: Yellow   Element: Earth for balance

                      Yoga posture associated with late summer: Ustrasana

Late in summer the spleen and stomach need greater attention. Focus on relating more, breathing deeply and meditating on a daily basis. Avoid being resistant to change or eating while nervous or stressed out. This may cause imbalance and create further problems.

AUTUMN
Characteristics: Color: White   Element: Metal for communication
Yoga posture associated with Autumn: Supta Baddha Konasan

Autumn is the time of year where the days become shorter and there is less sunlight in our lives. It is a time for the body to prepare for the winter rest period. Staying clear in all aspects of your life (mentally, physically, emotionally and spiritually) will make this seasonal change in transition easier.

Nutrition: Since the lungs and large intestine are associated with the autumn months, stay balanced and avoid stress. Remove or work on any addictive behaviors or negative habits that have been pulling you down. Be vitally aware of how your body reacts to food, its effect on mood and how well it is eliminated. Concentrate on increasing those foods which are helpful to enhancing the body's system and functions. For example: You notice that sugar and a high intake of fluffy white bread cause you to feel bloated, give you a headache and/or cause constipation. Remove them for two weeks and see if there is any change. Choose: Root vegetables, squash, pumpkins, any harvest vegetable or fruit, brown rice, almonds, mushrooms, and garlic. You will notice soups and casserole type dishes are more appealing in the fall. Increase fiber with apples, whole grains, and bran. Increase vitamin A with beets and carrots. Increase acidophillis for natural occurring intestinal bacteria which helps to increase absorption of nutrients and release toxins (found in most yogurts). Avoid too much sugar and flour (even whole wheat flour). Constipation is a signal that there is stress, so take the time to slow down and reduce the onset of it.

CHECK YOUR BALANCE
Balanced: Put order to emotions, physical things and the physical body. Create good communication with yourself and those around you. Increase rest time and quietness. Do special things to care and nurture yourself.

Out of Balance: Overindulgence, fatigue, wastefulness, confusion, living in any type of painful situation.

WINTER
Characteristics: Color: Blue   Element: Water for emotions
                              Yoga posture associated with winter: Urdhua Mukha Savasana
   Nutrition: Decrease stress on the bladder and kidneys by drinking plenty of water. The diet should include: fish, beans, whole grains, pasta, brown rice, barley and oats. Most fruits are recommended except for berries because they are out of season. Vegetables are important as one tends to eat heavier, fattier foods. Enjoy equal amounts of food, work, rest and play.

CHECK YOUR BALANCE.
   Balanced: Listen to internal signals that come from a well rested state. Share a peaceful, quiet and warm homelife. Give in all ways.
   Out of Balance: Overactivity, lack of sleep, frustration, staying up too late.

MEDICAL TERMS

Deciphering Medical Jargon:

PRESCRIPTION TERMS:

qh	(quaque hora)	every hour
qd	(quaque die)	every day
bid	(bis in die)	twice a day
tid	(ter in die)	three times a day
qid	(quarter in die)	four times a day
prn	(pro re nata)	as needed
a.c.	(ante cibum)	before meals
p.c.	(post cibum)	after meals
P.o.	(per os)	by mouth
sig	(signetur)	label this
h.s.	(hora somni)	at bedtime
stat	(statim)	immediately

Knowing the following helps one to understand diagnostic terms:

INDICATION

AT THE BEGINNING

a-, an-	without, lacking
dys-	painful, difficult
gastr-, gastro-	stomach
hem-, heme-, hemo-	blood
hyper-	excessive, over
hypo-	diminished, deficient
hyster-, hystero-	uterus
myo-	muscle
neur-, neuro-	nerve
nephr-, nephro-	kidney

AT THE END

-algia, -dynia	pain
-ectomy	surgical removal of
-emia	blood
-genic, -genetic	caused by
-gram	picture, measure, tracing
-graph	recording instrument
-itis	inflammation
-oma	tumor, growth

-ostomy	surgical opening
-otomy	surgical incision
-plegia	paralysis
-rhage, -rhagia	sudden flow, discharge
-rhea	flow

Standard ratios required for food and manufactured foods: You may be surprised at some of the requirements.

MEAT	MUST CONTAIN AT LEAST...
Beef	

All beef or all pork	100% beef or pork
Lasagna with meat sauce	12% meat
Meat ravioli in sauce	10% meat in ravioli
	50% ravioli in product
Meat stew	25% meat
Chili con carne	40% meat
Ham spread	35% cooked ham
Meat sauce	6% meat
Meatballs in sauce	50% cooked meatballs

Poultry

Chicken chop suey	4% chicken
Chicken ala king	20% chicken
Turkey Fricassee	20% turkey meat
Turkey with gravy	35% turkey meat

Canned fruits and vegetables

Fruit cocktail	65% fruit
Grapefruit	50% grapefruit
Whole plums	50% plums
Crushed pineapple	73% pineapple
Corn	61% corn
Tomatoes	50% tomatoes

Fruit juice

Orange juice	100% orange juice
Orange drink	5% or must state "less than 5%"
Apple, cherry, or pineapple juice	100%
Prune juice	18.5% prune juice

APPETIZERS
AND
DIPS

Salsa

This goes well as a condiment or a dip for corn chips. You'll need:

4 ripe tomatoes, chopped (in winter use plum tomatoes)
2 jalapenos, minced
1 small can tomato sauce or 1/4 cup V8™
1 teaspoon garlic, minced
Salt to taste
2 tablespoons cilantro, chopped
1/4 cup onion, chopped
2 scallions, diced
Juice of 1 lemon or lime (optional)
1-1/2 teaspoon olive oil

Combine all ingredients and allow to sit overnight (refrigerated). This will keep for two weeks. Variation: Add cooked corn kernels.

Serves: 4   Calories: 47

Pineapple Salsa

This version of Salsa is great with grilled chicken. You'll need:

1 20-ounce can pineapple, crushed
Juice and grated peel of 1 lime
1/4 cup red pepper, minced
1/4 cup green pepper, minced
1/4 cup yellow or orange pepper, minced
1/4 cup scallions, chopped
2 teaspoons cilantro
2 teaspoons jalapenos

Drain juice from pineapple. Combine all ingredients. Refrigerate. Store in airtight containers until ready to use.

Serves: 4   Calories: 64

Spinach Dip

1 clove garlic, minced
1 10-ounce package frozen spinach, thawed and drained
1/2 cup plain nonfat yogurt or low-fat mayonnaise
1/3 cup Parmesan cheese
1/4 teaspoon salt and pepper
1 package Knorr's™ vegetable soup mix
Dash of cayenne pepper

Blend all ingredients until smooth in blender or by hand in a bowl. Cover and chill. Serve in a hollowed-out Multi-Grain Bread.

Serves: 6   Calories: 95

Hot Artichoke Dip

This is always a success for a company appetizer.

1/2 cup light sour cream
1/2 cup Hellmann's Light™ mayonnaise
1 can artichoke hearts, drained and chopped
**   (marinated can be used also)**
1/2 cup Parmesan cheese, grated
1 teaspoon lemon juice
1 teaspoon hot pepper (cayenne)

Stir all ingredients. Spread into an ovenproof dish. Bake at 375° for 30 minutes, until it is golden and bubbly.

Serve with toasted Pita Bread (p. 119) or your favorite bread with garlic powder sprinkled on top.

Yield: 2 cups   Calories: 90 per 2-tablespoon serving

Guacamole I

1 ripe avocado, mashed   **1/16 teaspoon cumin**
Juice of 1 lime   **Black pepper to taste**
4 teaspoons salsa   **2 teaspoons scallions, diced**
1/2 teaspoon salt   **1 teaspoon cilantro**

Mash all ingredients and place pit in the middle to prevent browning.

Serves: 4   Calories: 45

Guacamole II

Guacamole is great with all Mexican food. Keep the pit of the avocado in the center while storing, to prevent darkening.

2 teaspoons garlic, minced
1/2 cup Hellmann's Light™ mayonnaise
Juice of 1 lemon
1 very ripe avocado, peeled and sliced

In a blender, mix all ingredients until smooth. Chill.

Yield: 2 cups   Calories: 120 per 2-tablespoon serving

Shrimp Quiche Appetizer

This delicious recipe can also be used as a side dish. You'll need:

1 8-ounce package refrigerated biscuits, rolls, or phyllo dough
4-ounce can small shrimp
1 egg
3/4 cup half-and-half
1/4 cup minced scallions
1/2 teaspoon salt
1/4 teaspoon cayenne pepper
1/2 cup Swiss cheese, shredded
1 tablespoon coarse mustard

Spray a 12-muffin pan with cooking oil. Separate refrigerator biscuits and separate again into halves. Press them into the bottom and partially up the sides of each cup.

Divide shrimp evenly on the bottom of the shells.

In a bowl, beat eggs, half-and-half, onion, salt, cayenne, and mustard. Top each cup with about 2 tablespoons of mixture.

Sprinkle cheese on top and bake for 15 minutes at 375°.

Serves: 6   Calories: 247

Nachos with Black Beans

Nachos are tasty with chopped meat or chicken added, but try it this vegetarian way and see what you think. You will need the following:

1/2 cup dried black beans, prepared as per package directions
1 tablespoon olive oil
1 carrot, chopped
1 onion, minced
1 celery stalk, chopped
3 garlic cloves, minced
2-1/2 cups water
2 teaspoons thyme
1 teaspoon cumin, ground
1 teaspoon salt
1/2 teaspoon lemon rind, grated
1 teaspoon black pepper
1 teaspoon cayenne

In a large pot, heat oil over medium-high heat. Sauté onion, carrot, celery, and garlic for 4-5 minutes. Stir in beans, water, and spices. Bring to boiling; stir constantly.

Reduce heat to medium low and cook about 2 hours.

Serve hot with corn chips, Monterey Jack, or Cheddar cheese, sliced tomatoes, lettuce, onion, salsa, and guacamole.

Serves: 6   Calories: 88 (with chips and cheese, etc.: 470)

Vegetarian "Bluff" Rolls

These are wonderful for special occasions. You'll need:

Egg roll skins
1 bunch broccoli, chopped
1/2 pound Cheddar, grated
1/2 pound Mozzarella, grated
1 bunch scallions, sliced

Fill each skin as directed on package with broccoli, equal amounts of cheese and scallions. Fold and fry in canola oil until brown.

Drain on brown bags and serve with hot mustard and duck sauce (sweet and sour).

Servings: 1 each   Calories: 425

Elegant Crab Dip

Fresh vegetables can also be used for dipping. For this tasty dip, you will need:

1 package Knorr's™ vegetable soup mix
10-ounce package frozen chopped spinach, thawed and drained
8-ounce can water chestnuts, chopped
1/2 cup Hellmann's Light™ mayonnaise
1/4 cup plain yogurt
1/4 cup small-curd cottage cheese
1 can crabmeat, drained
Juice of 1 lemon
1 large round fresh loaf of bread

Mix all ingredients. Hollow out bread. Fill with dip, refrigerate, and serve.
(My favorite bread for this comes from Wyckoff Bakeries in New Jersey; it's a hearty oatmeal-topped bread.)

Serves: 8   Calories: 25 per tablespoon

Sankaty Crabmeat Wontons

Egg roll skins cut in quarters
1 can crabmeat
1 8-ounce package light cream cheese

Fill wonton with equal mixture of crabmeat and cream cheese.
Fry in canoli oil until golden.
Serve with honey mustard sauce.

Serves: 4 each   Calories: 90 per wonton; 360 per serving

Oysters Parmesan Appetizer

As I write this, Nantucket is currently farming oyster seeds in hopes of introducing them for a new marketable industry...

1 bunch scallions, chopped
1/4 cup fresh parsley, chopped
3 teaspoons garlic, minced
2 tablespoons butter
Juice of 1 lime
1 teaspoon Tabasco™
1/4 cup Parmesan cheese
1/4 cup bread crumbs
1/4 teaspoon back pepper
2 pounds oysters, washed and opened

In a skillet, warm butter over medium heat. Add scallions, parsley, garlic, lime juice, Tabasco, oysters, and cook 1 minute.

Remove from heat and add bread crumbs, cheese, and black pepper. Press on top of oysters. Broil for 3-5 minutes.

Serves: 4   Calories: 155

Steps Beach Sushi

1 package nori (seaweed) sheets
1 seedless cucumber, peeled (as you would an apple) and cut into strips
2 cups short-grain rice, cooked
2 tablespoons sesame seeds
2 tablespoons wasabi (Japanese mustard)
1 avocado, peeled and cut into slices
2 cups crab legs (imitation is best), sliced lengthwise
Sushi vinegar

Cook rice ahead of time; sprinkle sushi vinegar on it, and place in the refrigerator.

Take one nori sheet and place it on a cutting board. Spoon out rice evenly onto the sheet, about 1/4-inch deep.

Sprinkle sesame seeds on top. Lay out the cucumber, crab legs, and avocado on the sheet. Don't make it too thick. With a bamboo rolling mat or a heavy cotton placemat (dampened), roll up the sushi, squeezing as you go.

Cut with a sharp knife that has been placed under water.

Serve sliced sushi with a little wasabi and/or soy sauce on it. (Wasabi is a powdered mustard that is made by adding water. The longer it sits, the stronger it gets.) Makes approximately 4 rolls.

Use your imagination to design new kinds of rolls. Perhaps with scrambled egg, or fish eggs?

Serves: 4   Calories: 390

Cisco Sushi

Try this with smoked salmon, pork, smoked chicken...or combine them. You'll need the following ingredients:

1 **pound chicken breast, skinned, boned, and baked in foil 30 minutes, then sliced**
4 **ounces rice noodles, soaked for 5 minutes in warm water and drained**
1 **bunch watercress, washed**
1 **Chinese cucumber, cut into matchsticks**
1 **bunch scallions, chopped**
1/2 **cup pickled ginger, drained**
1 **avocado, cut into slices (sprinkle lemon juice on top to prevent darkening)**
2 **tablespoons sesame seeds**
2 **packages nori (seaweed) sheets**

Sauces:
Wasabi (Japanese horseradish)
1/4 **cup soy sauce**

On a cutting board place nori, layer lightly with chicken, noodles, watercress, cucumber, scallion, ginger, avocado, and sprinkle with sesame seeds. Roll into an ice cream cone shape, dip in sauce, and eat.

Serves: 6   Calories: 275

SOUPS

Potato Leek Soup

2 potatoes, cubed
Bunch of leeks, sliced
1 onion, chopped
Bunch scallions, chopped
1 teaspoon crushed garlic
Two 16-ounce cans chicken broth (or 1/2 broth, 1/2 water)
1 tablespoon olive oil or butter
2 cups milk
2 cups water
1 teaspoon salt
1 teaspoon pepper
2 tablespoons flour

In a small container, shake milk and flour together. Set aside.
In a large pot, heat oil with onion, scallions, and garlic until clear.
Add remaining ingredients except milk mixture; heat for 15 minutes.
Bring soup to a boil, add milk mixture to thicken, stirring constantly. Simmer longer if necessary and serve.
Other herbs to try in this soup: dill, cayenne pepper, thyme, parsley, or chives.

Serves: 4   Calories: 164

Cream of Parsnip Soup

2 tablespoons butter
1 medium onion, minced
1 pound parsnips, chopped
2 potatoes, chopped

6 cups chicken stock
1 teaspoon salt
1 teaspoon white pepper
1 cup half-and-half or low-fat milk

In a heavy pot, heat butter. Add onion and parsnips. Saute´ until soft.
Add chicken stock, potatoes, salt and pepper. Lower heat. Cover, and simmer for 45 minutes. Cool a bit.
In a blender, purée soup. Return to pot, blend in milk. Heat until hot, and serve.

Serves: 4 to 6   Calories: 93

Shrimp Chowder with Peppers

Use different peppers (jalapenos, chili, red, green, yellow) to make this soup interesting and colorful. It can be made as mellow or as hot as you want. Very simple and quick!

One 17-ounce can creamed corn
1/2 cup chopped onion
1 tablespoon margarine
1-1/2 teaspoon minced garlic
2 cups skim milk
1 cup water

1 chopped red pepper
1/2 pound medium shrimp
1/2 teaspoon red pepper flakes
1/2 teaspoon black pepper
2 tablespoons cilantro (optional)
2 tablespoons farmer's, goat or
    feta cheese (optional)

Saute´ onion and red pepper with the margarine until soft. Add corn, garlic, milk, shrimp, red pepper flakes, and black pepper. Simmer until shrimp is cooked through, about 15 to 20 minutes.

Crumble cheese on top (this adds approximately 10 calories per serving).

Great served with garlic pita bread or cornbread.

Servings: 6 (1 cup each)   Calories: 95

Albondigas (Mexican Stew)

Albondigas is a meal in itself. Serve with your favorite cornbread.

Make into meatballs (1 teaspoon each):

2 pounds ground beef
1/4 cup flour
1 egg

1/2 can chicken broth
Garlic, salt, pepper to taste

Set this aside and then, in a large pot, bring to boil:

3 cans beef broth or consommé
1/2 can chicken broth
4 cans water

Drop in meatballs and simmer, covered, for 5 minutes.

Add:
2 onions, chopped
1 bunch cilantro
3/4 cup rice
6 carrots, sliced
2 teaspoons oregano

1 bay leaf
1/3 teaspoon cumin
1 teaspoon chili powder
1 jalapeno, chopped
1 bunch spinach, coarsely chopped

Simmer 1 hour or longer; serve.

Serves: 10   Calories: 218

Hearty Cabbage Soup

Forget the salad and enjoy this soup with some whole-grain bread.

1 to 2 pounds beef short ribs
1 teaspoon vegetable oil
1-1/2 cup onions (2 medium), chopped
4 cups water
2 cans beef broth
1 ripe tomato, chopped
1 head cabbage, cored and sliced
3 tablespoons lemon juice or apple cider vinegar
2 tablespoons brown sugar
1/2 teaspoon pepper
2 tablespoons salt
1/4 cup raisins (optional)

In a large pot, brown ribs and onions in oil. Add remaining ingredients and simmer, covered, for at least 2 hours. Meat should fall off bones. Remove bones and serve hot.

To defat the soup further, cool in refrigerator overnight and skim off any surface fat.

Serves: 8   Calories: 62

Homemade Chicken Noodle Soup

Serve this soup with your favorite dark bread.

1 package chicken breasts, skinned and boned (approx. 2 pounds)
1 large onion, chopped
2 carrots, chopped
2 celery stalks, chopped
1 tablespoon garlic, chopped
1/3 teaspoon cayenne pepper
1 teaspoon pepper
6 cups water
1/2 cup noodles
Salt to taste (optional)
1 teaspoon coarse mustard

Spray a 2-quart pot with oil. Cube chicken and cook over medium-to-high heat with onion until brown.

Add all ingredients except noodles; cook over medium-low heat for 15 minutes.

Add noodles; continue to cook until noodles are done.

Sprinkle Parmesan cheese on top and serve.

Add a variety of different vegetables to make this dish unique each time it is served.

Serves: 8-10   Calories: approx. 100

Potato Watercress Bisque

3 cups chicken broth
2 potatoes, chopped
2 cups watercress, washed and drained
1/2 cup light sour cream
1/2 cup milk
1 teaspoon salt
1 teaspoon pepper
3 scallions, sliced

In a 3-quart pot, boil potatoes in chicken broth for 15 minutes. Cool.
Place all ingredients in a blender and mix.
Return to pot, stir over medium heat until hot.

Serves: 4   Calories: 184

Broccoli Soup

1 head or 2 cups broccoli, chopped
1 onion, chopped
2 cans chicken broth (13-1/2 ounces) or 1 large can
1 cup milk
1 cup water
1 to 2 tablespoons flour
1 teaspoon garlic
Pepper
1 tablespoon coarse mustard
Cooking spray

Place milk and flour in a blender and mix until smooth.
Steam broccoli and set aside.
Meanwhile, in a medium pot sprayed with cooking spray, glaze onions.
In the blender mix the broccoli with the milk and puree´. Add broccoli to the onions, along with the remaining ingredients, and heat until thickened.
Try substituting: cauliflower for broccoli, or mix them. Or use different vegetables: zucchini, squash, pumpkin. If time is a factor, omit blending veggies and just chop them well.
For **Cheese Broccoli Soup**, grate 1/2 cup cheddar cheese into soup while it's hot and stir.

Serves: 4   Calories: 63

Easy Borscht

This recipe makes enough for one or two people. Use with **Mock Sour Cream** (see below) for a richer flavor.

1 can beets with juice
1 onion, minced
1 carrot, minced
1 celery stalk, minced

1 teaspoon red wine vinegar
1 cup beef or vegetable broth
1 egg, hard-boiled (optional)

In a blender, process beets in their juice for 6 seconds. Add beef broth and vinegar, blend until smooth. Set aside.

In a pot sprayed with cooking spray, place onion, carrot, and celery; cook for 10 minutes at low heat until glazed, adding water to prevent sticking. Add beet mixture and heat for another 5 minutes.

Serve with 1 peeled hard-boiled egg in the middle and a teaspoon of **Mock Sour Cream**. Can be served hot or cold.

Mock Sour Cream

1/2 cup plain nonfat yogurt
1 teaspoon lemon juice

Drain mixture through cheesecloth, store in refrigerator overnight. Serve as you would regular sour cream.

Serves: 2   Calories: 60

Minestrone Soup

1 tablespoon oil or 2 tablespoons butter
1 large onion, diced
2 carrots, diced
2 celery stalks, diced
2 potatoes, diced
1/2 head cabbage (2 cups), chopped
1/2 pound or 1 (9 ounce) frozen package green beans
2 cans beef broth
1 16-ounce can tomatoes
1/2 teaspoon each oregano, basil
2 zucchini, diced
1 16 ounce (approximately) can cannellini (white kidney beans)
1 10-ounce package frozen spinach, chopped

In a large pot (8 quart) put in oil and next five ingredients. Cook until browned; then add remaining ingredients and cook for 1 hour in covered pan at low heat.

Yields: 20 cups   Serves: 10   Calories: approx. 89

Scallop Soup

Simple is best, and so is this soup. You'll need:

1/4 cup red pepper, diced
1 tablespoon butter
1 cup fresh spinach, washed and chopped
1 can (16-ounce) chicken broth
2 ounces Boursin cheese (garlic or pepper)
3/4 cup milk
1/2 pound scallops, shelled and washed
1/2 teaspoon salt
1/2 teaspoon pepper

In a pan, sauté red pepper in butter (about 5 minutes). Add remaining ingredients. Cook over medium heat for 10 minutes.

Serves: 2   Calories: 360

BREAKFASTS
AND
SNACKS

Summertime Granola

I love this in the morning with yogurt and fresh fruit; or it's great warmed with 1/4 cup skim milk and half a banana sliced on top. It is also wonderful alone, or as a topping for cobblers. Summertime Granola also makes a great gift, wrapped in pretty paper for the holidays. To make it, you'll need:

6 cups rolled oats
1/4 cup wheat germ
1/4 cup sesame seeds
1/4 cup Grapenuts
1/2 cup shredded coconut
1/2 cup dried cranberries or chopped dates
1 cup bran, oat bran, or bran flakes
6 ounces frozen apple juice concentrate
1/4 cup safflower oil
1/4 cup water
2 tablespoons cinnamon (optional)

1/4 cup chopped walnuts
1/4 cup chopped pecans
1/4 cup sliced almonds
1/2 cup raisins

Mix all ingredients except the raisins and dates in a large bowl. Place on two cookie sheets and bake in a preheated 325° oven for 35 to 40 minutes, stirring occasionally; it should be toasted, not burnt.

This Granola can be kept in an airtight container in the freezer or refrigerator until ready to use.

Serving size: 1/2 cup   Calories: 105 per serving

Jetties Morning Eggs

In a bowl, scramble 4 eggs (2 per person). Add 1/2 cup cottage cheese; 2 breakfast sausages, cooked and sliced; 2 tablespoons scallions (optional); salt and pepper.
Spray pan with cooking spray. Bake at 350° for 15 minutes or until done.
Serve with homemade muffins, biscuits, or toast.

Serves: 2   Calories: 210

Fun Mix

Don't let the calories scare you from trying this recipe. It is chock-full of "nuts" and nutrition. You will need:

1 package dried apricots (8 ounces)
1 package dried mixed fruit
1/2 cup seedless raisins
1/2 cup dates
1/2 cup unsalted cashews
1/2 cup sliced almonds
1/2 cup walnuts, chopped
1/2 cup unsalted peanuts
1/2 teaspoon cinnamon
1/8 teaspoon ground cloves

In a large bowl, mix all ingredients. You may want to cut up the dried fruits a bit more. When all ingredients are evenly coated with spices, transfer into airtight containers.

Serves: 6   Calories: 440

Ol' North Wharf Breakfast

In a greased baking dish, place:

A layer of diced potatoes (2 large potatoes)
A layer of ham or cooked bacon
A layer of Monterey Jack cheese

Make circles and place as many eggs as needed for serving. Cover with cream and bake at 350° for 30 minutes or until done.

Serves: 4   Calories: 543

Ol' South Wharf Grits

Cook 1 cup grits in pan according to package instructions. Make 4 holes for eggs. Top with salsa and cover. Cook until eggs reach desired consistency.

Other ideas: Add cheese; add vegetables such as broccoli, asparagus, zucchini, or spinach.

Serves: 2   Calories: 380

Swain's Wharf Cereal

3 cups rolled oats
1 cup Grapenuts
1/2 cup sliced almonds
1/2 cup oat bran
1/4 cup wheat germ
1/2 cup raisins
1 teaspoon cinnamon
4 teaspoons brown sugar (optional)

Mix all ingredients. Serve cold with milk, or hot.

For hot cereal, place in a greased pot: 1 cup cereal and 1 cup milk; top with 1 sliced banana. Simmer 10 minutes.

Calories: 190 per 1/2 cup serving

Straight Wharf Cereal in Crockpot

1/2 cup oatmeal (long-cooking)
1/4 cup cornmeal
1/4 cup millet*
1/4 cup rye flakes
1/4 cup barley
1/4 cup wheatberries* or sun-dried cranberries
1/4 cup (or to taste) dried apricots, sliced
1/4 cup dates, sliced
4 cups water
*Available at local grocery store or health-food store.

In a crockpot, mix all ingredients the night before. Use 1/4 cup of your favorite nuts, grains, or seeds, totaling approximately 2 cups. Add your favorite dried fruit, using more or less, depending on sweetness desired.

Add water in ratio of 2 to 1 with dried ingredients — i.e., 4 cups of water to 2 cups of dried ingredients.

Cook on low 6 to 8 hours. For longer cooking time, add 1 more cup water to prevent cereal being too dry. Add more or less water for consistency desired.

Serve with milk* or applesauce. Garnish with blueberries and slivered almonds, or your favorite fresh fruit.

*You can use any milk substitute — almond milk, soy milk, etc.

Yields: 6-7 cups   Serves: 6-8   Calories: 80

Rancheros

This recipe is great served morning, noon, or night!
You'll need the following:

1 16-ounce can refried beans with chilies
4 eggs
1/4 cup salsa (Miguel's™ from Stowe, Vermont, if you can't make it yourself)
1/2 cup shredded Cheddar or Monterey Jack cheese
2 flour tortillas*

Cover an iron skillet with cooking spray. Over low heat, cook beans and spread around the pan.

Make 4 holes and crack eggs into each hollow. Spread salsa evenly over the beans and then sprinkle cheese on top.

Cover the skillet and cook until eggs are cooked.

OR

Place iron skillet under the broiler until Rancheros are cooked.

*Tortillas can also be cooked at the bottom of the pan, but they get very dark. You can place them on top of the skillet when heated over the stove. Finally, you could place them in the oven for 5 to 8 minutes at 350°.

This recipe also goes well with bagels, toast, or corn chips.

Serves: 4   Calories: 250

MAIN MEALS

MAIN MEALS — SEAFOOD

Tips for preparing fish & shellfish

FISH

The 10-Minute Rule for Fish

Use this guideline when you bake (400 to 450°), broil, poach, steam or sauté, but not when you microwave or deep-fry.

1. Measure fish at its thickest point. Cook about 10 minutes per inch of thickness, turning fish halfway through the cooking time.
2. Add five minutes to the total cooking time for fish cooked in foil or sauce.
3. Double the cooking time for frozen fish that has not been defrosted.
4. To test for doneness, make sure fish flakes when tested with a fork. Perfect fish is moist and opaque or white in color.

How to Fillet a Fish

1. With fish lying flat, cut along the spine from the gills to the tail with a flexible boning knife.
2. Slide the blade between backbone and flesh, lifting the fillet away from the bone. Remove fillet. Repeat other side.
3. To skin, grasp the fillet by the tail, skin side down. Hold the knife at a slight angle and cut meat free.

SHELLFISH

SHRIMP

How to Clean Shrimp

1. With a knife, make a shallow cut from head to tail. Peel off shell and legs. (You can leave tail on if desired.) To devein, hold shrimp under cold running water. Pull or let the water rinse out the vein.
2. To "butterfly," cut along the back of the shrimp, about three-quarters of the way through. Spread the halves open.

Note: Raw shrimp turns pink and firm when done. It takes about 3 to 5 minutes to boil or steam medium shrimp in the shell. Watch it carefully.

CRAB

How to Crack a Crab

1. To remove back, hold bottom of crab in one hand and pry off the shell with the other.
2. Using a small knife, cut away gills. Wash off intestines and spongy material.
3. Break off claws and crack them with the handle of the knife or a mallet. Pry out the meat with a knife. Twist legs off of body, crack them, and remove meat.

4. Cut the body down the middle, then cut halves into several parts. Use the point of the knife to remove the lump of meat from each side and rear of the body.

5. Remove remainder of the meat by prying upward with the knife.

SCALLOPS, CLAMS

How to Open Scallops/Clams

1. Wash scallops or clams thoroughly, discarding any that have broken shells or have stayed open. Holding the scallop/clam in the palm of your hand (heavy gloves are a good idea), force the blade of scallop/clam knife into the shell halves.

2. Run the knife around the edge of the shell and cut through the muscles holding it together.

3. Open the shell and remove top shell. Cut scallop/clam free from the bottom shell.

Note: Scallops turn milky white when done. Bay scallops take 30 to 60 seconds to cook, sea scallops 3 to 4 minutes.

Hints for Cooking Shellfish

•Shucked shellfish (oysters, clams, and mussels) become plump and opaque when done. The edges of the oysters start to curl up.

•The shells of oysters, clams, and mussels will open when they are thoroughly cooked. Remove from the water as they open. Discard any shells that remain unopened.

•Boiled lobster turns bright red when done. Allow 20 minutes per pound. For broiled split lobster, allow 15 minutes per pound.

•Cooking time for crabs depends on cooking method. Sauteéd soft-shell crabs take about 3 minutes each. Steamed hard-shell blue or rock crabs take about 30 minutes.

Note: ALWAYS have water boiling first before submerging any shellfish.

Sanford Farm Seafood Stew

1/2 cup olive oil
8 garlic cloves, minced, or 4 teaspoons garlic, minced
1 large yellow onion, sliced
1 large leek, sliced
1/2 red pepper and 1/2 green pepper, sliced
10 ripe tomatoes, diced or 2 large cans whole tomatoes
1/4 cup fresh parsley
1/2 teaspoon oregano
1/4 cup fresh basil
1 bay leaf
1/2 teaspoon rosemary & 1/2 teaspoon marjoram
1 teaspoon red pepper flakes
1 cup mushrooms
1 quart fish stock
1 cup red wine or white wine
1 teaspoon anisette (optional)
Salt
1 pound clams, washed
2 lobsters or crabs
2 pounds shrimp
1 pound flounder, sole, or cod

In a large pot add oil, garlic, onion, and leek; cook over medium heat till glazed. Add the remaining ingredients, except seafood, and cook covered over medium heat for one hour, stirring occasionally.

Add seafood, cook another 20 minutes.

Remove bay leaf and serve in large crock bowls.

Variations: Have it John and Joanie style — omit oregano, basil, bay leaf, rosemary, and marjoram and add 1 teaspoon of thyme.

Servings: 8-10   Calories: approx. 270-320

South Shore Bluefish with Apples

2 tablespoons butter
1 medium onion, chopped
2 pounds bluefish fillets cut in chunks
    or
2 pounds shrimp, shelled and deveined
    or
2 pounds chix, chunked
2 Granny Smith apples, sliced
1 pound snow peas, washed, stems removed
2 tablespoons sugar or honey
2/3 cup coarse mustard
3/4 cup milk shaken with 1 tablespoon flour

In a large skillet, cook butter and onion until tender. Add fish and cook 5 minutes, turning so it doesn't stick.

In a bowl, combine milk mixture, mustard, and sugar. Pour over fish and stir. Add pea pods, and cook 5 minutes.

Serve over angel-hair pasta.

Servings: 4 or 6   Calories: 578 or 385

Monomoy Scampi

The veggies can be steamed on the side as well. You'll need:

1/2 cup olive oil or 1/2 cup butter
3 cloves garlic, crushed
Juice of 1 lemon
2 carrots, sliced
    or
1 bunch asparagus, chopped (my favorite!)
1 zucchini, sliced
1-1/2 pound shrimp, peeled and deveined
Salt, pepper

In a large skillet, heat oil, add all ingredients, and cook over medium heat about 5 minutes or until shrimp are pink.

Serve immediately over angel-hair pasta or rice. Top with Parmesan cheese and fresh parsley.

Serves: 8   Calories: 172; with 1/2 cup pasta, 252

Nantucket Newburg

This recipe is delightful with lobster, shrimp, or any other fish.

1 pound Nantucket Bay Scallops
1/4 stick butter
2 cups milk (reserve 1 cup in shaker jar)
1/4 cup flour
3/4 cup sherry
1 teaspoon pepper
1 teaspoon salt (optional)
1/2 teaspoon cayenne pepper

In a large skillet, melt butter. In shaker jar, shake 1 cup milk with 1/4 cup flour. Add this mixture to the skillet and all other ingredients. Cook over medium heat until scallops are done, about 10 minutes. Scallops should be white, not clear, inside.

Adjust Newburg sauce to desired thickness by adding more milk for thinner sauce or more milk and flour to thicken.

Garnishes:
   —Fresh chopped chives
   —Fresh parsley
   —Paprika
Use your own preference to enhance the dish with alternative flavors.

Serves: 4   Calories: 315

Surfside Shrimp

This dish is quick, easy, and delicious!

1-pound can plum tomatoes
2 tablespoons olive oil
1 tablespoon minced garlic (3 cloves)
3 basil leaves, crushed (1 tablespoon, dry)
1 teaspoon red pepper
1 teaspoon salt
1 teaspoon pepper
1 tablespoon sugar
16 shrimp, peeled, cleaned, and cooked

Heat oil, add tomatoes, other ingredients. Cook 10 minutes and serve over pasta or rice.

Serves: 4   Calories: 177

'Sconset Salmon

This recipe is best for the grill. Here's how:

4 to 5 salmon fillets
2 tablespoons ground ginger

3 tablespoons black pepper
1 teaspoon salt

Sprinkle the salmon with ginger, pepper, and salt. Grill as usual, about 5 minutes per side.

Sauce:
3 tablespoons butter
1 shallot, peeled and minced
1 tablespoon garlic, minced
1 small tomato, diced
1 cup red wine

2 teaspoons balsamic vinegar
1 cup chicken stock
1 teaspoon pepper
1 teaspoon salt
1/2 teaspoon cayenne

In a skillet, heat butter, add shallots, garlic, and tomato.
Add remaining ingredients and cook to the desired consistency, about 20 minutes.
Serve warm atop the salmon.

Serves: 4   Calories: 431

Steamers, Dionis Style

This is the original way to serve clams.

20 clams (steamers) in shells
1 cup water
1 cup dry white wine

In separate bowls:

1/2 cup melted butter clarified)
Slice of fresh lemon
Juice from steamers after cooking

Scrub clams in cold water. Put water and wine in a large pot. Bring to boil, add clams. Cook, covered, until they open. Discard the ones that do not open.
Serve immediately with butter, juice, and lemon for dipping.

Serves: 4   Calories: approx. 184

Codfish Park Cakes

This recipe makes a succulent appetizer or main dish. Serve with lots of fresh vegetables.

1/4 cup low-fat mayonnaise (Hellmann's™ is good)
1 pound cod, haddock, or flounder fillets
Juice of 1 lime
1/4 teaspoon salt
1/4 teaspoon cayenne pepper
6 tablespoons bread crumbs (reserve 4 tablespoons in bowl)
2 tablespoons celery, minced
2 tablespoons scallions, chopped
1 egg
1 tablespoon coarse mustard
2 teaspoons butter
1 teaspoon garlic, minced

Fill a large skillet with water. Bring to a full boil, then reduce to a simmer. Over medium heat, poach fillets for about 5 minutes, depending on thickness. Prick with a fork until they flake.

Add all ingredients, except 4 tablespoons bread crumbs and 2 teaspoons butter, in a large bowl, and mix with flaked fillets. Shape into 8 fish cakes.

Dredge in bread crumbs.

Heat butter over medium heat in skillet. Saute fish cakes for 3-5 minutes, until golden brown.

Serves: 4   Calories: 321

Miacomet Shrimp

2 pounds shrimp, cooked, peeled, deveined
1/4 cup (2 stalks) celery, chopped
1 onion, chopped
1 tablespoon butter
2 carrots, chopped
1 package chicken bouillon
1 cup buttermilk
1 cup milk
2 tablespoons cornstarch
2 tablespoons lemon juice
1 tablespoon curry powder
1/4 cup golden raisins or
   1/4 cup chopped apple

In a large skillet, melt butter, curry, carrots, water, and package of bouillon. Cook over low heat for 10 minutes.

In a bowl or shaker, mix milk, buttermilk, and cornstarch.

Add all remaining ingredients to saucepan. Stir for 2 minutes until shrimp turn pink.

Serve over rice.

Serves: 8   Calories: 310

Lightship Scallops and Grits

1 pound scallops, removed from shell, washed and drained
1 teaspoon salt
1 cup grits
2 teaspoons butter
1/2 cup Cheddar cheese, grated
2 slices bacon, cooked and diced (optional)
1 cup mushrooms, diced
1 bunch scallions, chopped
2 teaspoons garlic, minced
1 tablespoon parsley
Juice of 1 lemon
Dash Tabasco™
Pepper

Cook grits as per package directions. Blend in 1 teaspoon butter and the cheese. Dash the top with Tabasco.

In a skillet sprayed with cooking oil and 1 teaspoon butter, sauté scallops and mushrooms for about 4 minutes. Add scallions, garlic, parsley, lemon juice.

Serve over grits.

Serves: 4   Calories: 416

Shawkemo Egg Foo Yung

You can omit the shrimp and easily make this a vegetarian dish.

Pancakes:

6 eggs
1 cup fresh bean sprouts
1/2 cup cooked shrimp
4 scallions, chopped

1/4 cup fresh mushrooms
1 tablespoon soy sauce
1/2 teaspoon sugar
5 tablespoons oil

Beat eggs until light. Cut up shrimp and add to eggs. Beat in bean sprouts, scallions, mushrooms, soy sauce, sugar, and 1 tablespoon oil.

In a large skillet, heat remaining oil. Add a ladle of egg mixture. Flip as you would a pancake. Keep warm.

Sauce:

1 cup water
1 beef or vegetable bouillon cube
2 tablespoons each soy sauce and
   cornstarch, whisked together

2 tablespoons sherry
1/2 teaspoon sugar
1/2 teaspoon garlic, minced

Bring all ingredients to a boil in a saucepan. Reduce heat. Stir until thick.

Serves: 6   Calories: 610

Brant Point Scallops with Dumplings

This dish is a labor of love, well worth making.

Dumplings:

3 ounces salmon (smoked, fresh, or canned)
1/2 pound scallops (shelled, cleaned, and rinsed)
1 egg white
1 teaspoon dill
1 tablespoon lemon juice
1/4 teaspoon salt and pepper
1/3 cup milk
1 teaspoon flour

Fill a 2-quart pot two-thirds full with water and bring to a boil, then simmer over medium heat.

Meanwhile, mix all ingredients together in a blender. Start with the first six ingredients, then add the milk and flour and mix briefly. (Do not overprocess.)

Drop 1 teaspoonful of dumpling mixture into simmering water. Cook each dumpling for 2 minutes. Remove with a slotted spoon onto a tray. Use then or store covered in the refrigerator.

Scallops:

1 pound Nantucket Bay scallops, shelled and washed
4 tablespoons butter
2 tablespoons flour
2 tablespoons lemon juice
1 tablespoon fresh parsley, chopped

Toss scallops in flour.

In a large skillet, melt butter with lemon juice. Sauté scallops for 2-5 minutes over medium-high heat. Add dumplings and cook over medium heat for 2 more minutes, until heated through. Garnish with parsley.

Serves: 4   Calories: 420

Mock Clambake

You will need the following for this great meal:

2 pounds steamers (softshell clams), scrubbed
2 pounds littleneck or cherrystone clams, scrubbed
2 pounds mussels, scrubbed, black threads removed
2 pounds small red potatoes, washed and boiled for 2 minutes and then drained
4 ears of corn
4 lobsters (1-1/4-pounds)
4 pounds seaweed

In a 5-gallon steam pot, add two inches of water and a quarter of the seaweed.

Layer lobsters and seaweed, clams and mussels and seaweed, and finally corn and potatoes and seaweed.

Cover and cook 20 minutes over high heat until clams and mussels have opened and lobsters have turned red.

On a table, layer newspaper and place a large bowl in the center. Put out melted butter and lemon wedges. Serve equal portions on large plates and enjoy the feast!

Serves: 4   Calories: approx. 490 (without butter)

Quaise Cod

This is just as tasty with halibut or flounder. To make it, you'll need:

2 pounds cod fillets
1 egg
1/2 cup milk
1 cup Feta cheese, crumbled
1/4 teaspoon cayenne pepper
1 ripe tomato, chopped

1/4 cup pitted black olives, chopped
1/4 cup pine nuts
1 tablespoon scallions, chopped
1 tablespoon lemon juice
1 tablespoon parsley
1/8 teaspoon pepper

Preheat oven to 400°. Spray a 12 x 9-inch baking dish with cooking oil. Layer fillets on bottom.

In a small bowl, mix egg with milk. Stir in cheese, cayenne pepper, parsley, and lemon juice. Spread over fish. Sprinkle top with tomato, olives, pine nuts, and scallions.

Bake for 15-20 minutes.

Serves: 6   Calories: 377

MAIN MEALS — PORK

Easy and Different Pork Chops

This is an elegant in-the-woods meal. Simply cook it over a campfire. You'll need:

1/2 bottle Russian dressing
1 package onion soup mix
1 jar apricot fruit preserves
6 center cut pork chops

Mix first three ingredients.
In a baking dish, place 6 center-cut pork chops; top with mixture.
Bake, covered, for 1-1/2 hours at 350°.

Serves: 6   Calories: 307

All-in-One Pork Chop Dinner

This is an easy meal which needs nothing else, except your favorite beverage.

2 pounds pork chops (preferably boneless)
16 ounces sauerkraut
1 medium onion, sliced
1 Granny Smith apple, cored and sliced
4 potatoes, cubed
1 sweet potato, cubed (optional)
1/2 cup water
2 tablespoons brown sugar (optional)

Arrange pork chops on the bottom of a large baking dish.
Place onion, apple, and potatoes, and last the sauerkraut, over the chops. Add 1/2 cup water. Sprinkle sugar over top.
Cover with aluminum foil and bake at 400° for at least 3 hours (the longer the better).

Serves: 4   Calories: 360

Pocomo Pork

This recipe is an alternative to most grilled meats.

2-1/2-pound lean pork roast
1 cup cider vinegar
2 tablespoons Tabasco™
1 tablespoon Worcestershire sauce
1 teaspoon black pepper
1 teaspoon salt

In a small bowl mix cider vinegar, Tabasco, Worcestershire, pepper, and salt. Marinate roast in this overnight.
Cook 5 hours on grill with cover closed.
Cut into bite-sized pieces. Cook remaining marinade and toss with pork.

Serves: 6   Calories: approx. 365

Maxcey's Pond Moo Sho Pork

1 pound ground pork
1/4 cup sherry
1/4 cup soy sauce
1 tablespoon sugar
1 teaspoon salt
1 teaspoon pepper
1 tablespoon ginger, sliced (or 2 teaspoons ginger, powdered)
1 bunch scallions, sliced
2 garlic cloves, crushed
3 cups cabbage, shredded
1 can bamboo shoots, shredded
1/4 cup mushrooms, sliced
Flour tortillas (warmed)

Brown pork in a large skillet over high heat. Add remaining ingredients. Cook, stirring constantly, about 5 minutes.
Fill warmed tortillas with mixture.

Yield: 6   Calories: 286

Quidnet Giombotta

This delicious dish is included with the pork recipes because it contains sausage, but there's also chicken, and you can vary the meats you add or make it a vegetarian meal if you wish.

1 tomato, diced
8 ounces mushrooms, sliced
1 red pepper
1 green pepper
1 28-ounce can peeled tomatoes
1 can stewed tomatoes
2 medium potatoes, cubed
1 can artichoke hearts
1 can medium pitted black olives
2 large onions, sliced
1 pound hot sausage and 1 pound sweet sausage
1 pound chicken cut up in large pieces
1 tablespoon red cayenne pepper
1 tablespoon each salt and pepper

In a large 4-inch baking dish sprayed with cooking oil, add all ingredients. Cover with foil and bake for 3 hours or longer at 350°.

Serves: 8   Calories: 219

Pork Chops with Apricots and Prunes

This is an exceptionally tasty dish, one you can serve with pride.

Four 1-inch-thick pork chops
1 Granny Smith apple
1/4 cup each dried apricots and prunes
1 medium onion, chopped
2 yams, cut into 1/2-inch slices
1/2 cup apricot and rhubarb chutney
Cooking oil spray or 1/4 cup water

In a large iron skillet sprayed with oil, sear chops, browning on each side.
Spread top of each chop with chutney; add remaining ingredients.
Cover and bake for two hours at 350°.

Serves: 4   Calories: 340

Steamboat Calzones

This recipe is fun for teenage slumber parties along with a good-fun movie or video. You'll need:

1 frozen bread loaf, thawed
1 pound sweet Italian sausage, cooked (about 4 links)
2 green peppers, sliced
2 medium onions, sliced
8 ounces Mozzarella cheese, sliced

In a skillet, cook sausage with onion and pepper. Cut bread into 8 sections. Pull each of these into about 6 x 4-inch square. Fill with sausage, pepper, onion, and a slice of Mozzarella and seal edges to make a rectangular pocket.

Place on cookie sheet sprayed with oil. Spray the tops with oil.

Bake at 400° for approximately 20 to 30 minutes. Cut in half.

Use your imagination and fill with other ingredients, such as:

   —Chicken and Broccoli and Cheddar
   —Pepperoni and Ricotta and Mozzarella
   —Ham and Ricotta and Mozzarella
   —Mixed Vegetables

Serves: 4 (or 8 halves)   Calories: approx. 560 per pocket (280 per half)

MAIN MEALS — CHICKEN

Chicken Stew

2 cans stewed tomatoes (16 ounces each)
1 clove garlic, minced
1 medium pepper, sliced
1 medium onion, sliced
2 chicken breasts (whole, skinned and boned)
1 cup mushrooms, chopped
Salt and pepper to taste
2 tablespoons Parmesan cheese

Spray a pan with cooking oil. Cut up chicken and brown; add onion and pepper and cook chicken until soft.

Mix in tomatoes, garlic, and mushrooms. Cook for 10 minutes and serve over pasta or rice. Sprinkle Parmesan on top.

This recipe can also be baked, at 350° for 30 minutes.

Serves: 4   Calories: 264

Lemon Chicken

2 chicken breasts (whole, skinned and boned)
2 tablespoons Italian dressing
1/2 cup bread crumbs
Dry Italian dressing mix
Juice of 1 lemon

Cut up chicken into finger-sized strips. Brush a baking dish with Italian dressing.

Place 1 cup of the bread crumbs with 1/2 to 1 packet of Italian mix in a large plastic bag. Shake it up. Put chicken in the bag one piece at a time and coat with the bread crumbs.

Arrange chicken in dish. Saving a couple slices of lemon to garnish the dish, squeeze lemon juice over the top.

Bake at 450° for 20 minutes.

Serves: 4   Calories: 248

Honey Ginger Chicken

3 tablespoons honey
1 teaspoon finely shredded orange peel
1 tablespoon orange juice
2 teaspoons sodium-reduced soy sauce
1/4 teaspoon ground pepper
1/8 teaspoon ground ginger
2 whole chicken breasts, skinned and halved lengthwise
   (total weight 1 pound)

In a small mixing bowl stir together honey, orange peel, orange juice, soy sauce, pepper, and ginger.

Place chicken on the unheated rack of a broiler pan. Broil 4 to 5 inches from the heat for about 8 minutes, or until chicken is tender, turning once. Brush frequently with honey mixture during broiling.

Serve with rice and broccoli or asparagus.

Serves: 4   Calories per serving: 192

Chicken Pot Pie

1 package chicken breasts, skinned and boned
   (approx. 2 whole breasts)
2 carrots, sliced
2 onions, chopped
2 celery stalks, sliced
1 cup peas
2 tablespoons flour
1 cup water
1 tablespoon Bay's Seasoning™ or 1 bay leaf and 1/2 teaspoon each sage and thyme
1 tablespoon coarse mustard
1 cup low-fat milk
1 package low-sodium chicken broth
1 pie crust

Heat the oven to 350°.

Cube the chicken. Spray a large skillet with cooking oil. Brown chicken and 1 onion. Add 1 cup water and the vegetables. Cook 10 minutes at medium heat.

Add flour and milk together in a jar and shake. Stir into pan. Add final spices, stir for a minute or two.

Transfer into a pie dish that has been sprayed with cooking oil. Always remove bay leaf before serving! Bake 20-30 minutes.

Variation: Top with mashed potatoes instead of pie crust. Add cayenne pepper or Tabasco for a hotter pie.

Sweet yams make this dish wholly satisfying! (See page 109.)

Serves: 6   Calories: 253

Coatue Chicken

This is made with little fuss. You'll need:

2 tablespoons olive oil
2 chicken breasts cut in half (1 pound)
3 fennel bulbs, cut into 8 wedges
2 carrots, cut into large pieces
1 chicken bouillon cube
1 16-ounce can black beans
1 teaspoon pepper

In a large skillet add oil, and add chicken, and heat over medium heat until brown.
Add fennel, carrots, bouillon, pepper, and 1 cup water. Bring to boil and reduce heat to simmer for 20 minutes.
Stir in black beans, heat another 5 to 10 minutes, and serve.

Serves: 4   Calories: about 347

Chicken Chili for a Crowd

This is comfort food that is also FUN to eat! Make a batch and freeze what you don't use. You'll need:

1 package chicken breasts, skinned, boned, and cubed
  (about 1 pound)
1 large onion, chopped
1 large can peeled tomatoes
2 tablespoons garlic, chopped
1 can red kidney beans
1 can white kidney beans
1 can broth or dry packet (beef, chicken, vegetable, etc.)
1 cup water
1 tablespoon cayenne
2 tablespoons chili powder

2 tablespoons cumin
1 tablespoon salt/pepper
1 tablespoon sugar (optional)
1 teaspoon mustard (or use commercial packets of flavoring)

In a large pot, brown chicken, add onion while browning, and cook until clear. Stir to prevent sticking. Add remaining ingredients and cook for 15 minutes longer.
This recipe gets better with age. I prefer to cook it for 2 hours or more.
Serve with grated cheese, chopped onions, and Nacho chips.

Serves: 6   Calories: 216

Coskata Broccoli Stuffed Chicken

1 tablespoon oil
1 10-ounce package frozen chopped broccoli
  or
1 cup fresh chopped broccoli
1/2 cup bread crumbs
2 tablespoons Parmesan cheese, grated, or Feta cheese
2 stalks scallions, chopped
1/8 teaspoon pepper
2 whole chicken breasts, boned, skinned, cut in half
2 tablespoons flour
1 onion, sliced

In a bowl, mix broccoli, bread crumbs, cheese, scallions, and pepper. Set aside.
Spread open chicken breasts and pound to 1/4-inch thickness.
Place one-fourth of broccoli mixture in each breast; fasten with toothpicks, and flour pieces.
In a skillet over medium heat, heat oil and onion and brown chicken pieces for 12 minutes until tender.

Serves: 4   Calories: 305

Children's Beach Chicken

1 can sliced mushrooms
1 medium onion, chopped
1 garlic clove, chopped
1 tablespoon olive oil
2 chicken breast halves, chopped
1/2 teaspoon salt
1 teaspoon pepper
1/4 teaspoon parsley
1 28-ounce can whole peeled tomatoes

In a large skillet cook the chicken and onion in oil until brown. Add remaining ingredients. Serve over rice.

Serves: 4   Calories: 182; with 1/4 cup rice, 262

Hidden Forest Basil Chicken

This dish has a distinct taste that you'll love. To make it, you'll need:

1 small onion, chopped
4 chicken breast halves (2 whole), boneless and skinless
1/4 cup seasoned bread crumbs
3 tablespoons butter
1/4 cup milk
1 packet chicken bouillon
1 cup half-and-half
1/2 cup fresh basil leaves, washed and thinly sliced
1/4 cup Parmesan cheese, grated
1 teaspoon white pepper

Dip each piece of chicken in milk and then bread crumbs. In a large skillet over medium heat, melt butter. Cook chicken with onion until golden brown (about 10 minutes).

Remove chicken to a platter and keep warm. Add remaining ingredients to the same skillet over medium heat and cook about 10 minutes. If ingredients need to be thickened more, add 1 teaspoon flour to 1/4 cup water, shake, and add to mixture.

Pour sauce over chicken and serve.

Serves: 4   Calories: 340

Great Point Chicken

Enjoy crunching the healthy way!

4 chicken thighs, skinned
4 chicken breasts, skinned
1/2 cup plain yogurt
1-1/2 cup whole-wheat crackers, crushed
1 tablespoon fried chicken seasoning

Preheat oven to 425°. Spray a 13 x 19-inch baking dish with oil.

In a bowl, mix chicken with yogurt. Shake with crushed crackers mixed with seasoning in a plastic bag.

Bake 40 minutes until golden.

Serves: 4   Calories: approx. 445

Capaum Pond Cacciatore

Serve this Italian family feast with fresh bread and salad. You'll need:

1/4 cup flour
1 teaspoon salt
1 teaspoon pepper
3 pounds chicken pieces (skin removed)
1/8 cup olive oil
1 green pepper, thinly sliced
1 large onion, chopped
1 large can (14-16 ounces) whole peeled tomatoes
6- or 8-ounce can tomato paste
4-ounce can (or 1/2 cup fresh) mushrooms
2 cloves garlic, crushed
1/2 cup water
1/2 teaspoon basil and 1 teaspoon oregano (or 1 teaspoon Italian seasoning)
1 tablespoon sugar

In a plastic bag, combine flour, salt, and pepper. Place chicken in bag and shake, one at a time, to cover pieces.

In a large skillet over high heat, brown chicken in oil with garlic, peppers, and onions. Pour off fat.

Add remaining ingredients. Cover and cook 45 minutes over medium heat. Check intermittently to make sure it isn't sticking.

Serves: 4   Calories: 320

Second Point Chicken Divan

You'll need the following for this great main meal:

5 chicken breasts cooked, boned, and halved
3 packages broccoli spears, cooked
2 cans cream of chicken soup
1 cup mayonnaise
1 tablespoon lemon juice
1/2 teaspoon curry powder
4 to 6 ounces sharp cheese, grated
Buttered bread crumbs

In buttered baking pan, place 2 or 3 broccoli spears with 1/2 chicken breast on top.

Combine remaining ingredients and cover chicken and broccoli. Sprinkle with cheese and crumbs.

Bake at 350° for 25 to 30 minutes.

Serves: 8 to 10 people   Calories: 384

First Point Chicken

A taste of the Southwest in minutes. You'll need:

1/2 cup fresh cilantro, chopped
2 Serrano peppers, cored, seeded, and chopped
1/4 cup olive oil
2 teaspoons coarse mustard
1 teaspoon sage
1/2 teaspoon salt
2 plum tomatoes, chopped
Juice of 1 lime
6 scallions, sliced
4 chicken breast halves (2 whole), boned, skinned, and pounded flat

In a small bowl mix cilantro, peppers, oil, mustard, sage, and salt. Press chicken pieces into mixture one at a time.
In a skillet over medium-high heat, cook chicken 1-2 minutes each side. Remove and keep warm.
Add lime juice to skillet and cook scallions and tomatoes over high heat for 1 minute.
Top chicken with mixture and serve.

Serves: 4   Calories: 328

Lobster Shack Chicken Stew

This recipe is supposed to have come from a retired sea captain in memory of the spices of his seafaring days. You'll need the following:

3 whole chicken breasts, halved, skinned, and boned
2 onions, chopped
1 green pepper, cut into strips
1 red pepper, cut into strips
3 cloves of garlic, crushed
2 teaspoons curry powder
1/2 teaspoon turmeric
1 large can tomatoes, crushed
1/3 cup raisins

Spray a skillet with cooking oil. Over medium-high heat, cook chicken, garlic, pepper, and onions for 4-6 minutes.
Add remaining ingredients. Simmer over low heat 30 minutes.
Stir occasionally.

Serves: 6   Calories: 233

Harborside Chicken

This dish is very tasty, and has a unique flavor. You'll need:

1 onion, chopped
2 garlic cloves, chopped
1 pound chicken breast, boned, skinned, and cut up
1/4 cup green pepper, minced
1 large can whole tomatoes
1 teaspoon dried thyme
1 teaspoon paprika
1/2 teaspoon salt
1/2 teaspoon fresh basil, chopped, or dried
1/2 teaspoon pepper
1 teaspoon Tabasco™
1 cup zucchini, sliced into matchsticks
2 teaspoons cornstarch
2 teaspoons water
2 cups rice, cooked (set aside)

Coat skillet with cooking spray. Add oil and cook onion and garlic over high heat for 1 minute. Add chicken and cook 5 minutes. Stir constantly.

Add all ingredients except cornstarch and water. Cook 10 minutes over medium-low heat, covered. Shake water and cornstarch; add to skillet, and cook, stirring, 5 more minutes.

Serves: 4   Calories: 320

Widow's Walk Chicken in Phyllo

This dish can be altered and used as a side vegetable by omitting the chicken...or try fish. You'll need:

1 package frozen phyllo dough, thawed
1 package frozen spinach, thawed
1 package (8 ounces) Feta, crumbled
8 ounces Ricotta cheese
1/4 cup scallions, chopped
3 whole chicken breasts, cut in half, skinned, and boned

Preheat oven to 375°.

In a skillet sprayed with cooking oil, add scallions, cheeses, and spinach. Mix together, cooking about 2-3 minutes.

Separate phyllo sheets into 3-5 layers thick.

Place 1 half chicken breast on top of sheets, top with spinach mixture, fold and seal. Do the same to remaining half-breasts.

Arrange all 6 in pan sprayed with oil and bake 20-30 minutes.

Serves: 6   Calories: 335

Washing Pond Fajitas

Filling a flour or corn tortilla with a variety of fillings is a Southwestern convention. For this treat, you'll need:

2 pounds chicken (boned and skinned) or beef (sliced)

Marinade:
2 tablespoons olive oil
Juice of 1 lime
2 teaspoons garlic, minced
1/2 teaspoon cumin, ground
1/4 teaspoon salt and pepper
1 tablespoon fresh cilantro, chopped (optional)

Mix all ingredients. Marinate chicken or beef overnight.

Cut up:
1 each red, green, yellow pepper
2 large onions (sliced)

Jalapenos, sour cream, chopped tomato, grated cheese, scallions, as desired (see below)

In a large skillet, over high heat, sauté peppers, onions, and chicken or beef. Serve in heated tortillas with: minced jalapenos, sour cream, chopped tomato, fresh cilantro, grated cheese, chopped scallions, etc. Use your imagination.

Serves: 4   Calories: 457

MAIN MEALS — BEEF

Pot Roast

Pot roast is always better and easier to slice if cooked a day ahead.
You'll need the following ingredients:

1-1/2 pound boneless round or rump roast (rump tastes better, although you must defat* it)
2 large onions, chopped
2 tablespoons garlic, chopped
1 can or packet low-sodium beef broth
1 to 2 cups tea
1 tablespoon pepper; salt to taste

In a 4-quart pot sprayed with Pam, brown roast on all sides. Add onions and cook until glazed or clear. Water can be added to prevent sticking. Stir in remaining ingredients and cook for 2-1/2 hours.

Cool. Remove 1 cup of liquid to make gravy. In a covered jar, shake 1 cup of liquid to 2 tablespoons flour until smooth. Remove roast from pan and slice. Add flour mixture to pan and heat, stirring constantly, until thick.

*To defat rump roast, place lettuce leaves in liquid while cooking. The leaves draw out the fat. Remove them from the pot. After you have cooled the roast, scoop off fat that has settled on top of liquid.

Variations:
— Add celery, carrots, and potatoes to roast the next day. Cook for 20 minutes.
— Add prunes to roast while cooking it — or try mushrooms.

Serves: 4   Calories: 330

Quarterboard Beef Roast

1/4 cup coarse mustard
2 teaspoons garlic, minced
1 4-pound rib-eye roast, boneless
1 teaspoon tarragon

Preheat oven to 350°.
Mix mustard, garlic, and tarragon together.
Place roast in a large roasting pan and spread mixture on top. Cook about 1-1/4 hours.

Serves: 8   Calories: 415

Pimney's Point Pot Pie

2 pounds chuck roast, cut into 1-1/2 inch cubes
4 tablespoons flour
6 onions, cut into quarters
4 carrots, sliced
1 potato, diced
1 stalk celery, diced
1/2 cup peas
2 tablespoons oil
1 tablespoon parsley, chopped
2 cloves garlic, chopped
1/2 teaspoon ground red pepper
Salt and pepper
1 cup water

Preheat oven to 375°. Coat beef with flour and brown it in oil in large frying pan. Add onions; brown 10 minutes.

Stir in 1 cup water, carrots, potatoes, celery, peas, and spices. Cook 10 minutes.

Shake flour with 1 cup water. Add to pan to thicken.

Place mixture in pie pan sprayed with cooking oil and top with refrigerator pie crust or biscuit dough.

Serves: 6   Calories: approx. 359

The Grey Lady Skillet Supper

This is a quick and easy supper that will satisfy everyone! You'll need:

3 cups elbow macaroni, cooked
1 pound lean ground beef
1 cup onion, diced
1 clove garlic
1 8-ounce can tomato sauce
1 cup water
1 cup tomato paste
1 tablespoon sugar
1 teaspoon each salt and pepper

In a skillet on medium-high heat, cook onion and beef until browned. Drain off excess fat.

Add all ingredients except macaroni. Cook over medium heat for 20 minutes. Add macaroni, heat through, and serve. You can top with cheese.

Serves: 6   Calories: approx. 239

Gibbs Pond Beef

This is an easy one-dish meal. Your ingredients:

1 loaf frozen white bread dough, defrosted
1-1/2 pound lean ground beef
1 small onion, chopped
1/2 cup fresh mushrooms
1 8-ounce can tomato sauce
2 tablespoons ketchup or tomato paste
1/8 cup red wine
1/4 teaspoon each oregano, thyme, basil, parsley, salt, and pepper
1 egg, beaten
2 tablespoons Parmesan cheese, grated

In a large ovenproof skillet, brown beef, onions, and mushrooms over high heat. Drain any excess fat and add tomato sauce, tomato paste, wine, seasonings. Simmer over low heat, 15-20 minutes.

Divide bread dough into about 20 pieces and place evenly over beef. Let rise 30 minutes. (You may have some bread left over.)

Brush with egg and top with Parmesan. Bake uncovered at 375° for 30 minutes.

Serves: 6   Calories: 520

Beef Wellington

This is a classy dish that is sure to please any entertaining celebration. You'll need:

1 pound fresh mushrooms, diced
2 tablespoons butter
1/4 cup red wine
2 teaspoons garlic, crushed
Salt and pepper

In a skillet, melt butter over medium to high heat. Add garlic, mushrooms, wine, salt, and pepper and stir for about 3 minutes. Remove from heat and set aside.

4 filet mignon, approximately 1/4 to 1/2 pound each
1/2 pound liver paté (gourmet shop brands are good)
1 package pastry or phyllo dough (thawed)

Cut dough to fit around filets.

Spread filets with paté, top with mushrooms, and seal. Place seal-side down on cooking sheet sprayed with oil.

Bake at 375° for 50 to 60 minutes or until meat thermometer inserted registers 140°.

Serves: 4   Calories: 350

Veal Scallopini

Eat this and enjoy, with a lot less fat! You'll need:

1/2 cup corn meal
1/2 teaspoon black pepper
1/4 teaspoon cayenne pepper
4 veal scallopini, pounded thin
1/2 cup buttermilk
1 tablespoon olive oil
1 tablespoon butter + 1/2 teaspoon butter
1 tablespoon parsley, chopped
4 lemons, sliced thin
1/2 cup ripe tomatoes, chopped
Juice of 1 lemon

Place corn meal, black pepper, and cayenne in a plastic bag.
Dip veal in buttermilk and then shake in bag.
Melt oil and 1 tablespoon butter in skillet. Brown veal 2 minutes on each side. Set aside.
Remove any oil in skillet. Place lemon juice, parsley, 1/2 teaspoon butter, and tomato slices in skillet. Cover and cook 1-2 minutes. (Don't let it stick.)
Place 1 lemon slice over each scallopini and pour sauce over.

Serves: 4   Calories: 285

Wauwinet Shishkabab

2 pounds sirloin tips
1 red onion, peeled and cut in chunks
4 large cloves of garlic, peeled
1 red pepper, cut in chunks
1 yellow pepper, cut in chunks
1 green pepper, cut in chunks

You can also use chicken or sausage, cut up, for this dish.
Alternate meat, onion, and pepper on skewers. Marinate overnight in Teriyaki Sauce (p. 137) or your favorite salad dressing or the following:

Marinade:
1/2 cup orange juice
1 tablespoon garlic
2 tablespoons Worcestershire sauce

Grill until done, turning skewers. About 10-15 minutes total.

Serves: 6   Calories: 363

Tom Nevers Taco Pie

This is a one-dish alternative to individual Nachos. You can also make this with chicken or vegetarian style.

1 cup Nacho chips, crushed
2 pounds lean ground beef, cooked and drained
1 package taco seasoning
2 cups shredded Cheddar cheese
1 ready-made pie crust
1 can refried beans
1 cup lettuce, shredded
1 tomato, diced
1 small onion, minced

Bake pie shell for 10 minutes at 450°. Layer beans, meat, cheese, and Nacho chips. Repeat. Bake for 20-25 minutes. Top with lettuce, tomato, and onion. Serve with guacamole and sour cream.

Serves: 6   Calories: 415

MAIN MEALS — VEGETARIAN

Vegetarian Tortillas

4 wheat tortillas
1 (16-ounce) can refried beans

Heat tortillas in foil. On the stove, heat up refried beans from a can and add:

1 tablespoon dry wine
Dash cumin
Dash chili powder
2 tablespoons tomato sauce or V8™ juice

Simmer for 1/2 hour.
Place beans on tortilla on a plate, add lettuce, onion, **Salsa** (page 33), **Guacamole** (page 34) and shredded cheese. Serve warm.

Serves: 4   Calories: 173 each

Oriental Pasta with Vegetables

8 ounces angel-hair pasta

Prepare the pasta al dente and drain. Then mix the following ingredients except the soy sauce in a sauce pan:

2 tablespoons salad oil
2 cloves garlic, minced
1/4 teaspoon red cayenne pepper powder
2 carrots, sliced
1/4 cup water
1/4 cup pea pods
1/2 pound mushrooms, quartered
1 bunch scallions, chopped
1/4 cup soy sauce
1/4 teaspoon ginger

Heat these for 17 minutes; stir in soy sauce. Toss with pasta, and serve warm or cold.
Additions: chopped red cabbage, toasted sesame seeds, precooked chicken or shrimp.

Serves: 6   Calories: 108

Maddequecham Lasagna

For this recipe use packaged noodles or make your own. See Manicotti (p. 90).

8 ounces lasagna noodles
1 small onion, chopped
1/2 pound mushrooms, sliced
3 small zucchini squash, thinly sliced
4 carrots, sliced
1 cup spinach, chopped
6 ounces Monterey Jack cheese, shredded
2 cups cottage cheese or ricotta
1/4 cup green onions or chives, finely sliced
2 eggs (optional)*
1/3 cup Parmesan cheese (optional)
1/2 teaspoon salt
1 garlic clove, crushed or minced
1/8 teaspoon each oregano, basil, and thyme
1 cup tomato sauce

If using eggs, recipe contains one-third egg per serving

Boil and drain noodles.

Steam onion, mushrooms, zucchini, and carrots in small amount of water until tender. Add 1 cup chopped spinach and continue cooking until spinach is warmed. Add spices.

In separate bowl, mix cottage cheese, green onion, and eggs.

In 13 x 9 x 2-inch pan, layer noodles, vegetable mixture, cottage cheese mixture (spooned on top of vegetables into two 2-inch strips), grated Jack cheese, and then Parmesan cheese if using Parmesan, and tomato sauce. Repeat this step, ending with cheeses to obtain a crispy, brown top layer.

Bake uncovered at 375° for 40 to 50 minutes or until top is slightly browned.

Serves: 4   Calories: 450

Polpis Pizza

This recipe makes 4 pizzas — freeze what you don't use. You'll need:

Dough:

4 packages yeast
3-1/2 cups warm water
6 tablespoons olive oil
4 teaspoons salt
2 teaspoons basil
2 teaspoons oregano
9-1/2 to 10 cups flour

Set flour aside. Dissolve yeast in water. Mix in remainder of ingredients, except flour.

Stir in half the flour. Add remaining flour to form a slightly sticky dough. Knead for 10 minutes. Raise in a warm place (oven for 1-1/2 to 2 hours).

Punch down and spread evenly onto 4 greased and floured pizza pans or cookie sheets.

Ladle on sauce; add cheese and desired topping. Cook in hot oven (450°) for 20 to 30 minutes.

Quick Sauce (if you don't have time to make sauce): Simmer for 1 hour, covered, the following:

2 small cans stewed tomatoes
1 small can tomato paste
1 tablespoon garlic
1 tablespoon sugar

Topping:

3/4 pound grated Mozzarella
3/4 pound grated Provolone

Or try sauteed mushrooms, onions, and peppers. You can make this a non-vegetarian meal by adding pepperoni, sausage, etc. Try anything!

Serves: 8 per pizza   Calories: approx. 178 each slice

Madaket Manicotti

1 16-ounce package Ricotta cheese (part skim)
1 16 ounce package part skim Mozzarella cheese (shredded)
1 egg
1 teaspoon Italian Seasoning (optional)

Mix all ingredients together. Use filling in the homemade egg noodles (see below). Roll about 3 tablespoons in each pancake. Top with tomato sauce.

Noodles for Manicotti and Lasagne

6 eggs
1 cup flour
1 cup milk

Beat all ingredients together until smooth. Fry in a greased pan as you would a thin pancake. Stack the noodles and set aside until ready to use.

Serves: 8   Calories with sauce: 343

Eel Point Pasta

This recipe is easy to prepare and has virtually no fat. You'll need:

8 ounces mushrooms, sliced
4 ripe tomatoes, diced
2 cans (or 10 ounces frozen) artichoke hearts, chopped
1 cup white wine
1 cup chicken broth (or vegetable broth if you're a strict vegetarian)
1 tablespoon balsamic vinegar
1 tablespoon olive oil
Salt and pepper
1 pound angel-hair pasta

In a 6-cup saucepan, heat oil over medium heat, add garlic, and cook 1 minute.
Add all the remaining ingredients except for pasta. Stir over medium heat for 10-15 minutes.
In a large pot filled with water, cook pasta in boiling water as per package directions. Drain.
Toss broth mixture with pasta and serve immediately with Parmesan bread sticks.

Serves: 4   Calories: 133

Squam Delight

This is a great high-carbohydrate meal.

1 bunch escarole lettuce, washed and leaves separated
2 teaspoons garlic, minced
2 tablespoons olive oil
Water
1 teaspoon salt
2 ripe tomatoes, chopped
1 large can cannellini (white kidney beans)
2 cups cooked tricolor pasta
Red pepper to taste
2 tablespoons Parmesan cheese, grated

In a large skillet, heat oil and garlic. Add 2 tablespoons water and escarole and sauté for 5 minutes. Then lower heat and simmer for 15 more minutes. Stir in remaining ingredients.

Serves: 4   Calories: 320

Sheep Pond Enchiladas

Here is a scrumptious casserole dish that can be made a day ahead.

1 onion, minced
2 tablespoons garlic, minced
1 can (16 ounces) black beans
2 tablespoons fresh cilantro, chopped
2 teaspoons cumin powder
4 tablespoons olive oil
1 10-ounce jar enchilada sauce
12 corn or flour tortillas
2 cups Cheddar cheese, grated

In a medium saucepan, over medium heat, sauté onion and garlic with 2 tablespoons oil. Mix beans, cilantro, and cumin into sauce and leave heat on low.

In a large skillet, heat 2 tablespoons oil and enchilada sauce. Heat tortillas one at a time on each side. Set onto a paper towel.

Spread beans on tortillas. Top with cheese. Roll up and place in a pan sprayed with cooking oil. Top with enchilada sauce and remaining cheese.

Bake at 350° for 20 minutes.

Variation: When serving, top with peanuts, sour cream, scallions, etc.

Serves: 6   Calories: 582

Jackson Point Tamale Pie

Chopped meat can be added in place of beans to transform this into a nonvegetarian meal.

Filling:

1/2 teaspoon olive oil
1/2 cup red pepper, chopped
1/2 cup green pepper, chopped
1 small jalapeno, chopped (approx. 1 tablespoon)
1 10-ounce package frozen kernel corn
1 large onion, chopped
1 19-ounce can red kidney beans
1 15-ounce can stewed tomatoes
6 ounces vegetable juice cocktail
1 tablespoon cilantro, chopped
2 teaspoons chili powder
1 teaspoon cumin powder

In a large skillet, heat oil over high heat. Add onion, red and green peppers. Sauté until soft.
Stir in remaining ingredients and cook over medium heat for 5 minutes.
Place filling in a 2-quart casserole dish that has been sprayed with cooking oil.
Heat oven to 375°.

Topping:

1 cup yellow or blue corn meal
1/2 cup flour
1 tablespoon sugar
2 teaspoons baking powder
1 teaspoon salt
3/4 cup buttermilk (or 3/4 cup milk with 1 teaspoon vinegar added)
1 egg
1 tablespoon cannoli oil
1/2 teaspoon pepper, ground

In a large bowl, mix all dry ingredients. Stir in all liquids — milk, oil, and egg — until combined. Pour over vegetable filling.
Bake 35-40 minutes.
Other Ideas: Grate 1/2 cup Cheddar cheese over vegetables before topping with cornmeal.
Add dollops of sour cream over vegetables before adding cornmeal topping.
(Both of the above additions are high in fat.)

Serves: 8   Calories: 198

Nobadeer Noodles

This makes a tasty side dish to meals. You'll need:

8 ounces angel-hair pasta
4 scallions, chopped
3 tablespoons rice vinegar
1/4 cup peanut butter
1 tablespoon hot chili oil
1/4 cup sesame oil
1/4 cup safflower oil
2 tablespoons sesame seeds
1 cucumber, peeled and sliced in thin sticks
1 tablespoon soy sauce
Salt and pepper to taste

Combine vinegar, peanut butter, all oils, and soy sauce together. Mix well.

Cook the pasta al dente.

Toss pasta and mixture together in a bowl. Top with scallions, sesame seeds, and cukes. Toss lightly. Sprinkle with salt and pepper. Serve warm or chilled.

Serves: 6   Calories: approx. 217

HOLIDAY MENU IDEAS

NEW YEAR'S DAY

Ring in the New Year with:
- Shrimp Chowder with Peppers
- Capaum Pond Cacciatore
- Fresh Salad with Homemade Croissants
- Garlic Parmesan Toast
- Cheesecake

VALENTINE'S DAY

Be someone's favorite Valentine and serve:
- Caesar Salad
- Beef Wellington
- Braised Red Cabbage
- Candied Sweet Potatoes
- Strawberry Creme Tart

ST. PATRICK'S DAY

Enjoy sharin' of the green with:
- Hearty Cabbage Soup
- Pocomo Pork
- Sweet Yams
- Boston Cream Pie, Nantucket Style

EASTER/PASSOVER

Make the most of the blessings of Springtime with:
- Easy Borscht
- Quarterboard Beef Roast
- Potato Pancakes
- Steamed Green Beans*
- Carrot Cake
  Not included

95

MOTHER'S DAY

Treat mother to a breakfast in bed!
- Fresh coffee/tea
- Summertime Granola
- Yogurt and fruit
- Fresh juice

FATHER'S DAY

Fathers love to eat — make their day with bluefish that they caught:
- Fresh salad (any dressing)
- South Shore Bluefish with Apples
- Tunnel of Fudge Cake

4TH OF JULY/SUMMER CELEBRATIONS

Three cheers for summer picnics and cookouts!
- Pasta Salad
- Wauwinet Shishkabobs
- Grilled Corn
- Baked Beans
- Braised Vegetables
- Krumkake (filled with ice cream)

HALLOWE'EN

There's no trick to treating yourself to:
- Scallop Soup
- Widow's Walk Chicken in Phyllo
- Broccoli Salad
- Chocolate Chip Cookies

And of course cider! Here's a "bonus" recipe for a great Hallowe'en cider

Mulling Spices for Cider

2 teaspoons allspice

2 teaspoons cinnamon

2 teaspoons sweet orange peel

1/2 teaspoon star anise

2 teaspoons cloves

2 teaspoons nutmeg

In a cheesecloth, add spices; tie it shut and mull for at least 1 hour in juice, wine, or tea.

THANKSGIVING

Give thanks and celebrate the bountiful feast.
- Maple Cranberry Sauce
- Turkey and Mother's Secret Stuffing
- Acorn Squash with Apples

CHRISTMAS/CHANUKAH

Make the season joyous! Take your time and enjoy an evening of:
- Sankaty Crabmeat Wontons
- Nantucket Newburg
- Fresh Salad with Walnut Dressing
- Biscuits
- Rice Pudding
- Pecan Turtles (to give as gifts)

IDEAS FOR CHILDREN'S BIRTHDAYS

- Polpis Pizza (Have the kids help make it.)
- Fun Mix
- Nachos with Black Beans
- Apple Barbecue Sauce on Chicken
- Strombolis
- Krumkake (Shaped into cones and filled with Fun Mix)
- Chocolate Chip Cookies (Let the kids bake them.)

ENTERTAINING IDEAS

- Have the children design their own T-shirts, hats, or tablecloth with fabric crayons or acrylic paints.
- Candy necklaces: Use shoestring licorice and thread fruit-flavored circular candies or tubular licorice onto it. Tie ends.
- Have a breakfast party, using many of the yummy recipes in the Breakfast section.
- Put pancake mixture in a squirt bottle and squeeze to form your name on griddle.
- Decorate the birthday cake with:
  — jellybeans
  — building blocks or other toys
  — edible flowers

WEDDING IDEAS

Nantucket is probably the ultimate spot for a wedding.

Shower Theme Ideas:
— sporting goods
— color theme
— crafts
— special interest
— gardening

Edible Flowers for the Wedding Food Decorations:
— carnations, chrysanthemums, dandelions, day lilies, marigolds, squash flowers, violets, daffodils, nasturtiums, pansies

Theme Weddings:
— nautical
— beach party
— barbecue/cookout

TEATIME

Nantucket is the perfect place to embrace the 4:00 hour with teatime. Here's how to make it a celebration:

To Brew the Perfect Cup

1. Warm the pot, fill it with hot water, and set aside.
2. Fill an empty kettle with cold, fresh water and set to boil. Fresh water is aerated.
3. Empty the warmed teapot and add one teabag per person.
4. As soon as the water boils, fill the teapot slowly and stir gently.
5. Cover and let stand 3 to 5 minutes. Set on a tea warmer/cozy.

What to Do

If tea is too strong...add more hot water to the pot.
If tea is too weak...make sure tea has stood long enough. If it's still weak, it's best to start over.

Milk, Lemon, and Sugar

• When using lemon, stir in sugar first so that the citric acid doesn't prevent the sugar from dissolving.
• Use milk, never cream, because cream masks the flavor of the tea.
• The British Standards Institute states that milk should be poured into the cup before the tea. The reason? Hot water will scald the milk and will enhance the tea flavor.
• The British do not recommend sweetening your tea. But if you must, use one or two lumps of white sugar rather than brown sugar.

Tea Biscuits or Scones

Biscuits and scones make perfect partners for tea.

Try lemon poppyseed, plain, ginger, or orange scones. A variety of biscuits such as oat, cheese, bran, and wafers are suitable choices as well.

Iced Tea

1. Prepare hot tea.
2. Add sugar, if desired, and cool.
3. Add ice cubes and chill.
4. Add lemon or a sprig of mint and serve.

PICNIC IDEAS

The Perfect Picnic

Picnics are simply wonderful on Nantucket Island. The key to planning the perfect picnic is to include foods that will keep safely. Here are some helpful hints:

• Make food ahead of time.
• Chill thoroughly before adding to coolers, or vice versa for hot foods.
• Do not pack hot and cold items together.
• Once at your destination, keep food out of direct sunlight.

A Checklist of What to Take on Your Picnic:

Picnic blanket	Bottle opener
Umbrella	Grill/lighter fluid/charcoal
Thermos	Paper towels/premoistened towels
Knives, spoons, forks, napkins	Camera
Condiments	Insect repellent
Garbage bags	Matches
Plates and bowls	Ice
Serving utensils	Candles
Glasses or cups	Marshmallows

...OH...some more? Yes, "S'Mores"!

Chocolate bar and Graham crackers, of course! (Try roasting your marshmallows, then putting them along with a thin slice of tart apple and a square of a chocolate bar between two Graham crackers. The best outdoors dessert ever!)
ENJOY!

And Speaking of Picnics... Here are some Nantucket Specialties...

A GAM

What's a gam? It's a tailgate party enjoyed after a game. Originally it referred to whales sporting in the water; later it came to mean getting together to socialize. And what better place for a gam than a picnic?

(continued)

A RANTUM SCOOT

Probably derived from the term "random scoot," a rantum scoot on Nantucket has come to mean setting out with all your picnic gear with no particular destination in mind — you'll know it when you find it!

A SQUANTUM

On the other hand, a squantum is a picnic whose destination is preselected — perhaps some secret, quiet, beautiful island spot.

VEGETABLES

VEGETARIAN CUISINE

Many people claim to be vegetarians. However, there are many different types. Here are what they mean:

Vegans: Diet includes grain, nuts, seeds, vegetables, fruits. No dairy, eggs, meat, fish, or poultry.

Lacto-Vegetarian: Vegan diet including milk and dairy.

Ovo-Vegetarian: Vegan diet plus eggs as the only source of animal protein.

Lacto-Ovo-Vegetarian: Vegan diet plus milk, dairy, and eggs.

Zen Macrobiotics: Diet consists of only brown rice and herb tea.

Fruitarians: Eat only fruit, nuts, seeds, honey, and olive oil.

Oesco-Vegetarians: Permit fish, but no other animal products.

Pollo-Vegetarians: Allow poultry as the only animal protein.

Red Meat Abstainers (partial vegetarian): Allow all animal products except for red meat.

One concern with the true vegan diet is that it may be deficient in complete protein. Therefore, I have included a chart to show what foods make up complete or complementary proteins.

COMBINATIONS FOR COMPLETE PROTEINS

Grains + Legumes

brown rice + beans

whole-wheat pasta + peas

low-fat cornbread + beans

taco salad + beans

tortilla + beans

whole-grain bread + peanut butter

brown rice + split-pea soup

burrito + beans

rice + lentil soup

Grains + Dairy/Eggs

wheat germ + low-fat yogurt

rice + low-fat cheese

macaroni + low-fat cheese

whole-grain cereal + low-fat milk

whole-grain bread + low-fat melted cheese

Grains + Vegetables

COMBINE these **vegetables** with a **grain**. For example:

asparagus

broccoli

Brussels sprouts

cauliflower

snap green beans

collard greens

lima beans

okra

peas

spinach

corn + peas

corn + lima beans

rice + broccoli

bread + collard greens

Legumes + Nuts/Seeds

soybean curd (tofu) + sesame seeds
tofu + almonds with cooked vegetables
tossed salad with beans + sunflower seeds

peanuts + sunflower seeds
bean soup + sesame crackers

Legumes + Dairy/Eggs

beans + low-fat cheese
lentil soup + low-fat milk
spinach salad with almonds + chopped egg

nut topping + low-fat plain yogurt
chili + low-fat grated cheese

Legumes + Vegetables

COMBINE these **vegetables** with a **legume**. For example:

beet greens
collard greens
kale
mustard greens

sweet potato
Swiss chard
winter squash
yam

three-bean salad + yam
lentils + acorn squash
black-eyed peas + mustard greens

Nuts/Seeds + Dairy/Eggs

pecans + low-fat cottage cheese

chopped almonds + low-fat cheese ball

Vegetables + Dairy/Eggs

potato salad (with egg and yogurt)
mashed potato + milk
broccoli + low-fat cheese
spinach + cheese
tossed salad + grated cheese

potato + low-fat cheese
vegetable + omelet (may use egg substitute)
spinach salad + sliced egg
cucumber + yogurt
tossed salad + yogurt-based dressing

FRUITS AND VEGETABLES
AT THEIR PEAK

Summer
Apricots, beets, berries, cherries, corn, cucumbers, grapes, mangos, melons, nectarines, okra, peaches, pears, peas (snap), peppers, plums, summer squash, tomatoes

Fall
Apples, avocados, Brussels sprouts, cauliflower, celery, cranberries, eggplants, papayas, pears, potatoes, pumpkins, sweet potatoes, turnips, winter squash

Winter
Broccoli, cabbage, celery, Chinese cabbage, eggplants, grapefruit, greens, oranges, parsnips, peas (late winter)

Spring
Artichokes, asparagus, bananas, cabbage, carrots, greens, peas (early and snap), peppers, pineapples, rhubarb, strawberries

FIBER FACTS

Fiber plays an important role in our everyday diets. Fiber prevents constipation, reduces the risk of hemorrhoids, helps to lower blood cholesterol levels, reduces the risk of diverticulosis, may help prevent some types of cancer, increases the amount of time it takes to eat (so you don't overeat), softens the stool (for easier elimination), and helps in the absorption of nutrients and elimination of toxins. Whew! So how do we get more fiber in our diets? Here are some suggestions:

- Use brown rice and whole-grain pastas
- Eat fresh whole fruits
- Use whole-grain products (breads, cereals, grains)
- Use a variety of raw vegetables in salads and as side dishes
- Introduce more legumes to your diet

What are good fiber foods? Here are a few:

Breads/Cereals: Bran, all bran cereals, whole-grain flatbreads (such as Norwegian flatbread), oatmeal, shredded wheat, barley, and the like.
Fruits/Nuts: Bananas, peaches, pears, apples (unpeeled), cherries, plums, raisins, peanuts.
Vegetables: Canned or home-made baked beans, canned or home-made refried beans, green beans, broccoli, Brussels sprouts, cabbage, corn, peas, potatoes, zucchini, carrots.

Note: While fiber is essential to the diet, too much can cause excess gas and bloating. Adjust your intake accordingly and enjoy the benefits fiber brings.

Stir Fry

2 cups pea pods
2 cups mushrooms, sliced

For a quick and easy stir fry, combine with 1/2 to 3/4 cup teriyaki sauce.
For a vegetable platter, add:

1 cup broccoli, chopped
1 cup sliced carrots

1 cup bean sprouts
1 cup cooked and cubed sweet potatoes

Again, all recipes are best when you apply your likes and dislikes to them. Experiment with a variety of vegetables or meats.

Serves: 8   Calories: 30

Sweet Yams

This side dish adds color and a bit of sweetness to your favorite meal.

2 pounds yams (6 medium)
1/4 to 1/2 cup orange juice
2 tablespoons maple syrup or brown sugar

1/2 teaspoon cinnamon
2 tablespoons butter
4 oranges

Wash yams and cut them up. Place them in pan and cover with water. Cook until tender, 30-35 minutes. Mash with all the ingredients except oranges.
Slice oranges in half. Scoop out pulp from oranges. Fill each half with mashed yams.
Sprinkle nuts on top. Serve warm.
Variations: Add molasses or brown surar to taste. OR mash with milk and maple syrup. OR add nuts, such as pecans or walnuts to taste. OR add 1 pound mashed baked potatoes with 1/2 cup milk and 1/4 cup butter (makes a fluffier texture).

Serves: 8   Calories: 110

Acorn Squash with Apples

This is a new way to eat squash!

2 acorn squssh (approx. 2 pounds each). Cut into 2-inch pieces. Do not peel.
3 apples, sliced
1 tablespoon brandy flavoring or 1/4 cup brandy
1 cup orange juice
2 teaspoons cinnamon
1/4 cup maple syrup
1/4 cup raisins

Place all ingredients in a large pot on stove. Bring to a boil and place on low heat for 1 to 1-1/2 hours, or until squash are tender.

Serves: 10 (1 cup)   Calories: 87

Turnip Bake

1-1/2 pound turnips, sliced
1/2 teaspoon thyme
1/2 cup Swiss cheese, grated
1 cup milk
1 tablespoon flour
8 very thin slices French bread
Salt and pepper

Preheat oven to 375°.

In a large pot, boil turnips for 5 minutes. Set aside.

Spray a 9 x 9 baking dish with oil. Place slices of French bread on the bottom and top with turnip slices.

In a bowl, mix milk with flour, then add thyme, salt, and pepper. Pour this over turnips and top with cheese.

Cover and bake 15 minutes. Remove cover and bake another 15 minutes until golden.

Serves: 4   Calories: approx. 212

Braised Vegetables

Serve this dish plain or over rice or pasta.

2 medium zucchini, sliced
2 medium yellow squash, sliced
1 medium onion, chopped
1 tablespoon olive oil
3 ripe tomatoes, quartered
1/2 cup canned corn

1/2 teaspoon oregano
1 teaspoon pepper
1 can stewed tomatoes
1 teaspoon minced garlic
1 teaspoon basil
1 tablespoon sugar (optional)

In a large skillet, heat oil over medium flame. Add onion and cook 5 minutes or until glazed and clear.

Add remaining ingredients and cook for 10 to 15 minutes. For a richer flavor, cook longer. For crisper vegetables, cook less.

Serves: 4   Calories: 85

Braised Red Cabbage

Tart yet sweet, this Lithuanian dish is best served with pork or ham. You'll need the following ingredients:

2 tablespoons butter
1 onion, chopped
1 head red cabbage, cored and cut into l/2-inch pieces
1 Granny Smith apple, cored and sliced
1/2 cup water
1/2 cup red wine vinegar (or apple cider)
1/8 cup each brown sugar and raisins
1/2 teaspoon salt
1/4 teaspoon ground pepper

In a 5-quart pot, melt butter; add onion and cook over medium heat for 5 minutes.
Add remaining ingredients. Cover and bring to a boil; reduce heat to low and simmer 45 minutes to 1 hour.

Serves: approx. 7 one-cup servings   Calories: 45

Candied Sweet Potatoes

This is a perfect way to curb your sweet tooth. You'll need:

5 pounds medium-size sweet potatoes or yams
Water
1/3 cup brown sugar or maple syrup
1/4 cup butter or margarine
1/2 teaspoon cinnamon

Cut potatoes lengthwise into quarters. Place in a large baking dish that has been sprayed with cooking oil. Add ingredients, cover, and bake at 350° for 2 hours. The syrup and butter will become syrup-like,
Top with shredded almonds.

Serves: 12   Calories: approx. 150

Island Succotash

This is great for lunch or as an accompaniment for broiled fish or meat. Island Succotash is a Nantucket tradition and still served in Plymouth to celebrate Forefather's Day, December 21. You'll need:

1 tablespoon olive oil
6 medium new potatoes (2 pounds)
1 green pepper, diced
1 red pepper, diced
1 onion, minced
2 tomatoes, chopped
1 10-ounce package frozen lima beans
1 10-ounce package frozen corn
1 16-ounce can kidney beans
3/4 cup water
2 teaspoons salt
1 teaspoon sugar
1 teaspoon pepper
1 tablespoon coarse mustard

Add oil to a 5-quart pot, cook onion and peppers over medium heat until soft. Add remaining ingredients.

 Cover and simmer for 20 minutes or more. The longer it simmers the more enhanced the flavor will get.

Serves: 10   Calories: 118

Pureed Beets

This dish complements potato salad very well. You'll need:

1 pound beets
1/4 cup walnuts
3 garlic cloves
1/4 cup fresh cilantro, chopped

1/4 cup fresh parsley, chopped
1/4 teaspoon coriander, ground
2 teaspoons red wine vinegar

Boil beets for 30 minutes.

In a blender, grind beets, walnuts, and garlic until mixed. Add remaining ingredients. Top with chopped hard-boiled egg (optional).

Chill and serve.

Serves: 6   Calories: 52

Low-Fat French Fries or Potato Chips

6 medium potatoes, sliced as fries
Cooking spray
Salt and pepper

Preheat oven to 450°. Spray cookie or baking sheet with oil, place potatoes on sheet and spray them with oil. Sprinkle with salt and pepper.

Bake 20-30 minutes or until golden.

For chips: Slice potato very thin and follow directions above. Bake 10-20 minutes.

Other ideas: Sprinkle with Parmesan cheese, garlic and pepper, onion powder, cayenne pepper, or soy sauce.

Serves: 6   Calories: 92

Moor's End Farm Broccoli

You can add many other vegetables to create variety!

2 tablespoons peanut oil
1 tablespoon ginger, chopped
1 head broccoli, chopped
1/4 cup beef or chicken bouillon

Heat oil in a large skillet on high heat. Add ginger. Cook 1 minute, then add broccoli and broth. Cook for 2 more minutes. Serve hot.

Serves: 4   Calories: 30

Bartlett Farm Grilled Corn

Prepared ahead of time, the corn is easy and delicious to have at a beach barbecue.

8 ears of corn
1/2 stick butter, melted

Heat coals on the grill. Place rack 4-5 inches above the coals.

Carefully peel back husks of corn, leaving them attached at base. Remove silk. Rinse corn and moisten husks thoroughly. Brush corn with melted butter and put husks back into place, covering kernels.

Grill corn 15-20 minutes, turning occasionally.

Serves: 8   Calories: 125

Garlic Rosemary Mashed Potatoes

6 potatoes
6 cloves garlic, minced
1-1/2 cup milk
2 teaspoons rosemary
Salt and pepper

Boil potatoes. Mash with remaining ingredients and serve.

Serves: 8   Calories: 130

Potato Pancakes

Potato Pancakes are wonderful with any meal, especially pot roast or turkey dinner. You'll need:

4 potatoes, grated
1/2 cup scallions, chopped
1 egg
1 teaspoon salt

1/4 teaspoon pepper
2 tablespoons flour
1/4 cup oil

Grate potato and add onion. Transfer to a bowl. Mix with egg, salt, pepper, and flour.

Heat oil in a skillet. Drop 2 tablespoons of mixture into skillet at a time. Flatten with a spoon to make two 3-inch pancakes. Fry 4-5 minutes.

Try adding leeks and spinach, corn, or vegetables.

Serves: 15   Calories: 175

Broccoli Puff

You'll need:

2 packages frozen chopped broccoli (or 2 cups fresh)
1 cup Bisquick™ or similar mix
1 cup milk
2 eggs
1/2 teaspoon salt
1 cup shredded Cheddar cheese

Preheat oven to 325°.

Butter 5-1/2-cup soufflé dish or 1-1/2-quart casserole.

Cook broccoli and drain.

Beat baking mix, milk, eggs, and salt by hand until smooth.

Stir in broccoli and cheese.

Pour into dish and bake until knife inserted comes out clean, about 1 hour. Serve immediately.

Servings: 8   Calories: 178

Baked Beans

2 tablespoons salad oil
1 large onion, chopped
1/4 cup Russian salad dressing
1/2 cup dark brown sugar
3 tablespoons coarse mustard

1/2 teaspoon salt
1 large can red kidney beans
1 large can baked beans
1 large can black beans
1 large can black-eyed peas

In large pot, add oil and cook onion in it over medium heat until tender, about 15 minutes.

Add remaining ingredients (you may adjust the sugar to taste) and cook for 1/2 hour over low heat, stirring occasionally. The longer it stands, the better the flavor.

Serves: 12   Calories: 163

BREADS
AND
MUFFINS

Pita (Pocket Bread)

1 cup lukewarm water (105° to 115°)
1 package active dry yeast
1 tablespoon sugar
Approximately 1-3/4 cup white flour
1 cup whole wheat flour
1 teaspoon oil
1 teaspoon salt

In a large bowl, mix water, yeast, and sugar. Let stand 5 minutes or until mixture bubbles. Add salt and oil. Gradually stir in 1 cup of white flour and 1 cup of whole wheat flour. Knead for 10 minutes, or until smooth and elastic. Place in a lightly greased bowl, cover, and let rise in a warm place for 1 hour.

Place dough on a floured surface and cut into 8 pieces. Make these in balls and flatten into 4-inch rounds. Let stand 10 minutes. Roll each ball out to 6 inches, about 1/4 inch thick. Place on heavily floured board and cover with waxed paper and a light towel. Let rise for 30 minutes in a warm place.

Meanwhile, place a heavy baking sheet in middle of the lowest oven rack, leaving 3 inches between sheet and oven walls. Preheat oven to 500°. After 20 minutes, carefully place risen rounds, floured side down, onto sheet with a very wide spatula.

Bake 4 to 5 minutes or until rounds look like balloons and are lightly browned. Remove onto waxed paper and cover with waxed paper and a towel. Cool, then press down to flatten.

Note: Red clay tiles can be used instead of a baking sheet. They will produce a lighter pita.

Serves: 16 (half pockets)   Calories: 83

Cranberry and Orange Oatmeal Scones

This is a quick recipe that is healthy, too! It is low in fat. You'll be proud to serve it for breakfast. Here are the ingredients:

1 cup unbleached flour
3 tablespoons sugar
1-1/2 teaspoon baking powder
1 teaspoon finely shredded orange peel
1/3 cup margarine or butter
1 cup oats
2 egg whites, slightly beaten, or 1 egg
2 tablespoons dried cranberries
2 tablespoons orange juice
Nonstick cooking spray
Milk

In a bowl, stir together flour, sugar, baking powder, and orange peel. Cut margarine into the flour mixture until small crumbs form. Add oats and raisins to mixture. Finally, combine egg whites and orange juice and mix all together.

Shape dough into a 6- to 7-inch circle. Spray baking sheet with nonstick coating. Place the scone on baking sheet and brush the top with milk.

Bake at 375° for 20 minutes.

This recipe can be fun. Just use your imagination and try different juices, add nuts, or change the grains. One of my favorites is lemon/poppy seed. For this, use lemon peel for orange peel, lemon juice for orange juice, and add 2 tablespoons of poppy seed.

Serves: 6   Calories: 62

Date Nut Bread

This recipe is great to give as a gift for the holidays in bread form, or you can make it into muffins. You'll need the following ingredients:

1 tablespoon margarine
1 package dates (8 ounces), chopped
1-1/2 cup boiling water
2 teaspoons baking soda

In a bowl, pour water over dates, soda, and margarine. Preheat oven to 350°. Add the following mixture:

1 cup brown sugar
1 egg or 2 egg whites
1-3/4 to 2 cups flour (whole wheat or unbleached)
1/3 cup wheat germ, oatmeal, or bran (or combination)
1 teaspoon vanilla

(continued)

Mix well. Sprinkle top with 1/4 cup slivered almonds or chopped nuts, after pouring mixture into greased bread pan; bake at 350° for 1 hour. Or you can pour into 12 greased muffin pans and bake at 350° for 30 minutes.

Serves: 15 (bread); 12 (muffins)   Calories: 140; 146

Stromboli I

This recipe makes a very tasty appetizer. You'll need:

2 loaves frozen French dough

Filling:

3/4 pound domestic Provolone cheese
3/4 pound Mozzarella cheese
3/4 pound sliced pepperoni (OR 1/2 ham and 1/4 pepperoni)

Spray loaves with cooking-oil spray and thaw (about 2 hours).

Stretch each loaf out individually in a long rectangle along the kitchen counter (approximately 24" x 25"). Line up cold cuts and roll into a long tube; circle it onto oiled cookie sheet.

Bake at 350° for 1/2 hour or until golden. Slice into serving portions and freeze unused slices in a plastic bag.

Serves: 12   Calories: approx. 248

Stromboli II

Same as above, but fill with:

3/4 pound Cheddar cheese, grated or sliced
3/4 pound Mozzarella cheese, grated or sliced
2 tablespoons scallions, chopped
1 small head chopped broccoli

OR...make up your own filling. Have fun.
This is great to serve with meals or use from the freezer as a quick lunch.

Serves: 12   Calories: approx. 198

Dark Bread

1-1/2 cup flour (1/2 white, 1/2 whole wheat)
1 cup rye flour
1/4 cup rolled oats
2-1/2 teaspoons baking powder
1-1/4 teaspoon salt
1/2 teaspoon baking soda
1-1/2 cup milk
1/2 cup dark brown sugar
3 tablespoons dark molasses
2 tablespoons vegetable oil
1 egg, beaten

Grease loaf pan. In a large bowl, mix milk, brown sugar, molasses, oil, and egg. Add flours, oats, powder, salt, and soda with fork until moistened. Pour batter into pan and let stand for 20 minutes.

Sprinkle top with 2 tablespoons oats. Bake 1 hour in preheated oven at 350°. Makes 1 loaf.

Serves: 10   Calories: 90 per serving

Taco Calzones Appetizers

1/2 pound ground beef
1/4 cup salsa or taco sauce
2 teaspoons chili powder
1/4 cup onion, chopped
1/2 teaspoon garlic powder
1/4 cup Cheddar cheese
10 ounces pizza dough or frozen bread dough

Preheat oven to 425°.

Over high heat, in a skillet, brown beef with onion and drain fat. Add remaining ingredients (except cheese) and set aside.

Stretch dough to about 14 x 11-inch rectangle. Cut into twelve squares.

Divide filling onto dough, sprinkle with cheese, and seal with the edge of a fork. Arrange on a baking sheet, sprayed with cooking oil. Spray tops of Calzones with oil and bake for 20-25 minutes.

Serves: 12   Calories: 130 per pocket

Good Morning Danish

Although this recipe is time-consuming at first, it will become a fun recipe to make again and again with different fillings. Also, it makes a great gift for friends and family and a wonderful holiday-morning breakfast.

Bottom:

1/2 cup butter, soft
1 cup flour (mix 1/3 cup each of wheat germ, whole-wheat flour, and all-purpose flour)
2 tablespoons water

Heat oven to 350°. Cut 1/2 cup butter with flour mixture until particles form. Sprinkle water over mixture and mix with fork. Gather into a ball, and pat down evenly onto a large cookie sheet into a rectangular form.

Filling (optional):

8 ounces cream cheese, softened
1 egg
1 teaspoon lemon
1/4 cup confectioner's sugar

Mix these together and evenly layer them onto the pastry.

Top puff:

1/2 cup butter
1 cup water
1 teaspoon vanilla or almond extract
1 cup flour
3 eggs

Heat 1/2 cup butter and 1 cup water and vanilla in a pan to a rolling boil. Remove from heat and quickly stir in 1 cup flour until mixture forms a ball.
Add eggs and beat until smooth.
Spread over rectangle. Bake about 1 hour. Let cool.

Glaze:

1-1/2 cup powdered sugar
2 tablespoons butter
1-1/2 teaspoon vanilla

Mix above, then stir in 1 to 2 teaspoons warm water until smooth. Spread Danish with glaze and sprinkle with nuts.

Serves: 8   Calories: 262 each

Biscuit Dough

2 cups flour
1/2 teaspoon baking soda
1/4 teaspoon baking powder

1/2 teaspoon salt
1/2 cup butter or solid shortening
3/4 cup buttermilk

Preheat oven to 350°.

In a bowl, combine flour, baking soda, baking powder, and salt. Cut in butter or shortening with knife until mixture resembles crumbs.

Add half the buttermilk, cut it into mixture with knife. Add remaining buttermilk until mixture forms into dough.

Spoon into pie, if you are using it as a beef stew topping, OR

Roll out on a floured cutting board, shape into a flat, round cake and roll to 9 inches in diameter.

Ease dough over beef stew; poke 3 holes in it. Bake for 20 minutes or until pastry is brown. Let pie settle for 5 minutes and serve.

If you are making biscuits (makes 12), cook for 20 minutes at 350° or until golden.

Serves: 12   Calories: 120 each biscuit

Croutons

Use leftover or fresh French bread, cut into cubes. Spray the pieces with cooking oil, sprinkle with garlic powder, and toast until golden.

Garlic Parmesan Toast

Garlic Parmesan Toast is great with soups! To make it, you'll need:

2 garlic cloves, minced
2 tablespoons olive oil
   or
3 tablespoons jarred garlic (minced, based in oil)
2 large Pita Pockets (see p. 119), sliced lengthwise and halved
3 tablespoons Parmesan cheese, grated
2 tablespoons fresh parsley, chopped (optional)

Preheat oven to 400°. Spread garlic and oil mixture evenly over bread.

Sprinkle Parmesan and parsley over bread and bake for 5 minutes or until golden brown.

Yield: 8   Calories: 72 each

Lemon Raspberry Streusel Bread

You can also make muffins with this recipe.

Streusel Topping:

3 tablespoons butter, softened
1/4 cup light brown or granulated sugar
1/2 teaspoon cinnamon
1/4 to 1/3 cup flour
2 tablespoons rolled oats

In a medium bowl, blend ingredients until mixture resembles crumbs. Set aside.

Bread:

1 stick butter, softened
1/2 cup granulated sugar
2 eggs
2 cups flour
1 teaspoon baking powder
1/2 teaspoon baking soda
Juice and grated rind of 1 lemon
1/2 cup light sour cream
1/2 cup milk
1 cup fresh raspberries

Preheat oven to 375°.
Spray a loaf pan with cooking spray and flour it lightly.
In a large bowl, cream butter, add sugar and eggs. Grate lemon into mixture. Cut lemon in half and squeeze into mixture.
Beat and add milk and sour cream until smooth.
Mix flour, baking powder, and soda. Sprinkle dry ingredients into wet ingredients. Beat remaining ingredients except for raspberries, until smooth (2 minutes).
Fold in raspberries, and turn mixture into loaf pan. Top with streusel and bake 45-50 minutes, until toothpick inserted comes out clean.
Sprinkle confectioner's sugar on top.

Serves: 12   Calories: 221

Rice Bread

This unique bread serves up well with fresh sautéed vegetables on top. You'll need:

3 cups well-cooked brown or white rice
1 teaspoon salt
1 cup milk
1 teaspoon honey
4 eggs, separated
1 cup Gruyere or Cheddar cheese, grated
1/2 cup Parmesan cheese, grated
1/2 cup flour
2 teaspoons baking powder

Preheat oven to 375°.
Mix rice, salt, milk, honey, and egg yolks. Add cheese, then flour and baking powder. Stir well.
Turn mixture into a shallow buttered 1-1/2 quart baking dish. Bake for 25-30 minutes, until golden.
Serve as a side dish or main meal with a variety of vegetables.

Serves: 6   Calories: 331

Multi-Grain Bread

This is a hearty bread packed with nutrition. To make it, you'll need:

3 packages dry yeast
2-3/4 cups warm water
4 cups flour
1-1/2 cup whole-wheat flour
1-1/2 cup oat bran flakes
1/2 cup yellow cornmeal

1/2 cup rolled oats
1/2 cup wheat germ
2 tablespoons flax seed or poppy seed
3 tablespoons honey
1 teaspoon salt

In a large bowl, sprinkle yeast into warm water. Let sit 5 minutes. Stir in remaining ingredients.
Place dough mixture onto floured surface. Knead dough for 10 minutes.
Wash bowl and spray with cooking oil. Place dough into bowl. Cover with a clean cloth and let rise for 45 minutes. (It should double in size.)
Spray a baking sheet with cooking spray. Form dough into a 4 x 8 rectangular loaf. Cover and let rise 45 more minutes (again doubling in size). Heat oven to 375°.
Score lines across the top of loaf. Brush with milk and top with oats.
Bake 50 minutes, until golden.

Serves: 12   Calories: 243

One-Pan Pancake

This is great served as a Sunday morning breakfast. You'll need:

1/2 teaspoon brandy flavor (optional)
2 tablespoons butter
3 pears, halved and cored
5 eggs, separated
1/2 cup sugar
1 teaspoon vanilla
1/4 cup flour (whole-wheat or white)
1/4 cup oats

Melt butter with brandy in skillet over medium heat. Place pears in skillet and cook until golden on each side. Set aside in skillet, and keep warm.

In a bowl, beat egg whites on high until foamy; then add sugar and beat until stiff.

In another bowl beat yolks, vanilla, flour, and oats.

Fold in egg whites and flour mixture over pears.

Cook in 300° oven for 15 minutes.

Variations: Try different fruits, such as peaches, apples, or a mixture of blueberries, raspberries, and strawberries. You can top with yogurt and toss a little Granola (p. 49) on it, too.

Serves: 6   Calories: 235

Rugelaeh

This is a classic Russian pastry. Enjoy it with afternoon tea, or for Jewish New Year.

Pastry:
4 cups flour
1 teaspoon baking powder
2 sticks butter
Two 8-ounce packages cream cheese (soft)

Mix all ingredients until well blended. Separate into two balls and refrigerate (covered in plastic) for 2 hours.

Roll into 14 x 6-inch rectangle.

Filling:
1-3/4 cup walnuts, chopped
1 tablespoon sugar
1 teaspoon cinnamon
6 ounces raspberry preserve or apricot spread (Sorrell Ridge™)

In a bowl, mix walnuts, sugar, and cinnamon.

Spread raspberry preserve onto rolled-out dough lengthwise. Roll lengthwise and slice into 1-inch pieces. (Optional: roll in 1/2 cup cinnamon mixed with 1-1/2 cup sugar).

Bake at 325° for 40 minutes.

Makes 14 pieces   Calories: 222

SALADS

Pasta Salad

You can serve this salad hot or cold. It's an easy traveler for the beach. You'll need:

1-pound box tricolor pasta
1/2 cup chopped red onion
1 to 1-1/2 cup broccoli, chopped
1/4 cup pepperocini (hot pepper rings), chopped
1 ripe tomato, cut in chunks
1 8-ounce package Feta cheese, crumbled
1/2 cup black pitted olives (optional)
1 cup Italian dressing (or dressing to taste)
6 tablespoons oil

Cook pasta al dente. Drain out the water and add all the ingredients.

Other vegetable ideas: carrots, scallions, zucchini, cauliflower, and artichokes, or sun-dried tomatoes.

Other dressing ideas: oil and vinegar, Greek dressing, Caesar dressing, or any fat-free dressing. Be creative and try various flavors! The salad lasts 5 days.

Serves: 12   Calories: approx. 163

Tortellini Salad

Again, this is an easy salad to make and keeps well. Its flavor is enhanced with age.

1 package cheese tortellini
1 package sun-dried tomatoes
1/2 cup oil
3 teaspoons minced garlic
1/2 cup chopped broccoli or cut-up spinach

Cook sun-dried tomatoes in water until hydrated. Drain and add oil and garlic, then set aside.

Cook pasta; add tomatoes and the green vegetable. Store in the refrigerator.

Serves: 4   Calories: approx. 210

Broccoli Salad

This recipe is very tasty, but higher in fat. Use it every now and again for summer get-togethers.

1 head broccoli, flowerets chopped
1/4 cup sugar or to taste
2 tablespoons vinegar
1 cup mayonnaise (or 1/2 cup light mayonnaise, 1/2 cup nonfat plain yogurt)
6-8 pieces bacon
1 small onion, minced

Bake bacon on a cookie sheet until crisp. (This keeps you from being splattered and gives you crisper bacon.) Set aside on a paper towel to drain excess fat.

In a large bowl, combine mayonnaise, sugar, vinegar, and onion. Stir until smooth. Add broccoli and onion mix, chill and serve.

Suggestion: You can also add cashews to this recipe. Again, very high in fat.

Serves: approx. 8   Calories: 216

Beet Salad

1/2 pound beets
1/2 cup walnuts
1/4 cup walnut oil or canoli oil
Juice of 1 orange
Juice of 1 lemon
Grated peel of 1 orange
1 orange, peeled and sectioned
1 head chickory lettuce
1 tablespoon honey
Salt and pepper

Cook unpeeled beets (stems removed) until tender, about 15 minutes. Cool and slice.

Mix well together the walnuts, oil, lemon juice, orange juice, orange peel, honey, and salt and pepper.

On four individual plates place sliced beets, orange sections, and lettuce. Drizzle mixture on top.

Serves: 4   Calories: 115

Summer Crab Salad

Bring on your summer picnics! This salad can be served as a hot dip also. Try it. You'll need the following:

1 pound fresh crabmeat, lumped and drained
1/4 cup celery, minced
2 tablespoons scallions, chopped
2 tablespoons plain nonfat yogurt
1/4 cup low-calorie mayonnaise
1 tablespoon white wine vinegar
1 ripe tomato, chopped
1 teaspoon hot sauce (Tabasco™)
1 teaspoon garlic, minced
1/2 teaspoon salt
1 teaspoon coarse mustard

In a large bowl, mix all ingredients. Chill and serve over lettuce.

Serves: 4   Calories: 275

Tuna Salad

Try using canned ham or salmon for this recipe too. You'll need:

1 can water-packed tuna
1 scallion, chopped
2 tablespoons small-curd cottage cheese
1 hard-boiled egg
1 teaspoon low-fat mayonnaise (Hellmann's™)
1 teaspoon coarse mustard

Mix all ingredients.

Serves: 2   Calories: 262

SAUCES
AND
DRESSINGS

Maple Cranberry Sauce

This sauce goes wonderfully with poultry or red meats. It is also a good alternative to use when making sandwiches.

12 ounces cranberries
1 cup diet cranberry raspberry juice
1 cup maple syrup
Grated orange peel
1/4 cup walnuts

In a saucepan, combine all ingredients. Bring to a boil, lower heat to medium, and cook until the cranberries pop, approximately 10 minutes. Skim off any foam that forms on surface. Cool and refrigerate.

Serves: 12   Calories: 92

Teriyaki Sauce

Use this in stir-fry recipes or as a marinade. You'll need the following ingredients:

1/4 cup cooking oil
1/4 cup soy sauce
1/4 cup dry sherry
1/4 cup honey
1 teaspoon ginger powder or 1 tablespoon fresh ginger root
1 clove garlic, minced
1 teaspoon cornstarch

Blend ginger, oil, soy sauce, honey, garlic, and sherry together in a bowl. (Use this as a marinade.)

For stir-fry recipes: Place ingredients in a pan over medium heat and add cornstarch. Sauce will thicken in a couple of minutes. Let cool and use for barbecues or as is for stir-fry. Sesame seeds go well over the vegetables.

Yield: 1 cup   Calories: 35 per serving

Vegetarian Tomato Sauce

3 tablespoons olive oil
3 cloves garlic, crushed
1 large can Progresso™* peeled tomatoes
1 18-ounce can Hunt's™* tomato paste
2 tablespoons oregano (approx.)
1 to 2 tablespoons sugar
1 tablespoon basil
2 cups water
Salt and pepper to taste

In a large pot, brown garlic in oil. Add 1 large can of the peeled tomatoes and all other ingredients, except for the tomato paste. Let simmer 20 minutes.

Add tomato paste and one can of water (use peeled tomatoes can for measuring) — this is approximately 2 cups. Simmer for at least 2 more hours.

*These tend to taste the best.

To add meat:

Brown sausage while browning the garlic. Always use 1 piece of sausage even if you are making other kinds of meat in your sauce, because sausage makes the best flavor.

1 pound of chopped meat can also be added.

Serves: 8 (1/2-cup each)   Calories: 43

Orange Ginger Dressing

1/2 cup fresh orange juice
2 teaspoons minced ginger or 1/2 teaspoon powdered ginger
3 scallions, sliced
2 tablespoons white wine vinegar
1 tablespoon lemon juice
1/2 cup olive oil
Salt and pepper to taste

Whisk together all ingredients except oil. Add oil slowly.
Serve at room temperature.

Yield: 1/2 cup   Calories: 52 per tablespoon

My Mother's Secret Stuffing

This stuffing has been kept a secret in our family for three generations. It is delightfully different and ever so GOOD!

1 16-ounce package of stuffing mix
1 apple, chopped
1 medium onion, chopped
1/2 to 1 whole dill pickle, minced
1 tablespoon Dijon mustard

1/2 cup water
1/2 cup celery, minced
2 teaspoons Bell's™ seasoning
4 tablespoons margarine

In a large skillet, melt margarine and add onion, apple, and celery. Cook until tender.
Add the rest of the ingredients and mix well.
Let the bread crumbs soak up the moisture and remove from stove.
When stuffing has cooled, you can proceed to stuff the turkey or chicken, or you can use it as a side dish as is.

Serves: 16 (1 ounce)   Calories: 100

Poppy Seed Dressing

This dressing is very tasty and will also make sauce for poultry or vegetables. You'll need:

2 tablespoons soft tofu
1/4 cup honey
1/4 cup sugar (or less, depending upon taste)
6 tablespoons tarragon vinegar or red wine vinegar
3 tablespoons lemon juice
1 teaspoon minced onion
1 teaspoon dry mustard
1 teaspoon paprika
1/4 teaspoon salt (optional)
2 teaspoons poppy seeds
1/2 cup salad oil (polyunsaturated)
1/2 cup water

Whisk together all ingredients except sugar and oil. Add sugar by the spoonful, until desired sweetness. Slowly add oil until desired consistency.

Yield: 2 cups   Calories: 80 per serving (2 tablespoons per serving)

Dilly Salad Dressing

This thick and creamy dressing also makes a great sauce for fish, poultry, or steamed vegetables. You'll need:

3/4 cup buttermilk, soft tofu, or low-fat plain yogurt
1/4 cup reduced-calorie mayonnaise or salad dressing
1 tablespoon tarragon vinegar
1 teaspoon sugar
1-1/2 teaspoon fresh dill or 1/2 teaspoon dry dill
Dash pepper

Blend all ingredients in a bowl or blender and chill.

Yield: 1 cup   Calories: 33 per serving

Mock Sour Cream I

Use this in place of sour cream for potatoes, salads, and other recipes. You'll need:

3 ounces low-fat plain yogurt
2 ounces low-fat cottage cheese
Squeeze of lemon

Blend and chill.

Calories: 45 per serving (2 tablespoons per serving)

Mock Sour Cream II

1/2 cup low-fat cottage cheese (small curd)
1/4 teaspoon lemon juice
1 teaspoon chives (optional)

Calories: 10 per serving (2 tablespoons per serving)

Zesty Garlic Dressing

This dressing is great as a marinade as well as a salad dressing. You'll need:

1 tablespoon cornstarch
1 teaspoon sugar
1 teaspoon dry mustard
1 cup cold water
1/4 cup vinegar
1/4 cup catsup

1 teaspoon horseradish
1 teaspoon Worcestershire sauce
1/2 teaspoon salt (optional)
1/2 teaspoon paprika
Dash hot sauce to taste
1 clove garlic, minced

In a small saucepan combine cornstarch, sugar, and mustard; gradually stir in the water. Cook over medium heat until thick and bubbly.

Remove from heat, and cover with wax paper for 10 minutes.

Stir in vinegar, catsup, horseradish, Worcestershire, salt, pepper, paprika, and hot sauce. Beat until smooth. Add garlic. Cover and chill.

Calories: 6 per serving (1 tablespoon per serving)

Apricot Sesame Dressing

1 teaspoon cornstarch
1/8 teaspoon garlic
1/8 teaspoon ground ginger
5-1/2 ounce can apricot nectar

1/4 cup red wine vinegar
1 tablespoon honey
1 teaspoon sesame oil
1 teaspoon sesame seed

In saucepan combine all ingredients. Cook 2 minutes, until thick and bubbly. Cool and serve. Toss over your favorite salad greens. This is very low-fat!

Serves: 6   Calories: 42

Walnut Dressing

This is a wonderful dressing on summer salads and lighter-fare meals. Try adding some apples, raisins, or grapes to the salad. You'll need:

1/2 cup sherry vinegar
1 cup walnut oil
1/4 cup olive oil
1 shallot, minced

1 teaspoon salt
1/2 teaspoon black pepper
1 tablespoon red pepper, chopped
1/4 cup walnuts, chopped

Place ingredients in jar; cover tightly and shake.

Yield: 2-1/2 cups (serves 16, 2 tablespoons per serving)   Calories: 80

Caesar Dressing

1/4 cup olive oil
2 tablespoons garlic cloves or 2 teaspoons minced garlic
1 anchovy

Blend the above, then add and blend:

1 tablespoon coarse mustard
Juice of 1 lemon
1 egg

Toss with salad greens with garlic croutons and 1/2 cup Parmesan cheese.
Garlic croutons: Cut up stale French bread. Spread it lightly with butter or margarine or spray with oil. Sprinkle on garlic powder and bake until golden.

Serves: 6   Calories: 58

Spicy Mustard Dressing

This dressing is great on salad or as a marinade for chicken. You'll need:

1 teaspoon minced garlic
1/4 cup hot spicy (coarse) mustard
1/4 cup lemon juice or vinegar
3/4 teaspoon white pepper
1/2 to 1 cup mayonnaise
OR, to defat, 1/4 cup olive oil and 1/4 cup light sour cream or nonfat yogurt

Try every way and see which you prefer. Whisk all the ingredients together in a bowl.

Yield: 1 cup (serves 10)   Calories: 68 per serving

Maple-Pear Glaze for Fish

1 small pear, chopped
2 tablespoons white wine
1 tablespoon shallot, minced
1/4 cup milk

1/2 teaspoon lemon peel, grated
2 tablespoons maple syrup
Dash allspice
Salt and pepper

Mix all ingredients together. In a saucepan, cook over medium heat, stirring constantly until mixture thickens. Use glaze on top of fish fillets.

Serves: 2   Calories: 258

Red French Dressing

6 ounces tomato juice
1 teaspoon catsup
2 tablespoons olive oil
1 tablespoon cider vinegar
1/2 teaspoon prepared coarse mustard
1/2 teaspoon Worcestershire sauce
1/8 teaspoon celery (chopped) or celery salt

Whisk ingredients together and serve.

Serves: 4 (2 tablespoons per serving)   Calories: 80

Pesto

In a blender, this is easy to prepare. You'll need:

2 cups fresh basil leaves, chopped
1/4 cup pine nuts
3 to 4 cloves garlic
1-1/4 cup olive oil
1/2 cup Parmesan cheese, grated
1/4 cup Romano cheese, grated
Salt and pepper to taste

In a blender, add all ingredients and mix until smooth (resembles creamed butter). Toss into your favorite pasta and serve. You can use warm linguine, for example.

The Pesto can be frozen in ice-cube trays and placed into a plastic bag until ready to use.

Variations: Adjust ingredients to suit your taste. You can add 1 tablespoon lemon juice; 1/4 cup parsley; 1/4 cup walnuts; or sun-dried tomatoes.

Another idea: Place cooked tortellini onto bamboo skewers and marinate in Pesto. Serve cold.

Calories: approx. 194 per 1/4 cup

Cajun Mix

2 teaspoons garlic powder
2 teaspoons onion powder
2 teaspoons paprika
2 teaspoons black pepper
3 teaspoons red cayenne pepper

Mix all ingredients. These spices go wonderfully on any fish, chicken, or beef. Sprinkle over meat on both sides and grill or broil in the oven.

Options:
— Spread small amount of mayonnaise on fish before sprinkling Cajun Mix
— Marinate chicken in oil/vinegar mixture before sprinkling on Cajun Mix

Elegant Ginger Garlic Sauce

Use over cooked shrimp, fish, chicken, steak, or pork chops, or even veggies. You'll need:

1/4 cup sliced scallions
1/2 teaspoon ginger root or ginger powder
1 clove garlic, minced
1 tablespoon oil
1/2 cup cold water
1-1/2 teaspoon cornstarch
1 tablespoon soy sauce
1 teaspoon oyster sauce (optional)

In a small saucepan cook scallion, ginger, and garlic in oil, stirring for 1 minute.
In a shaker bowl, add water, cornstarch, and soy sauce.
Add remaining ingredients to pan; cook and stir for 2 minutes. Serve hot over desired meat or veggies.

Yield: 3/4 cup   Calories: less than 20 per serving

Apricot and Rhubarb Chutney

This makes a great gift. Serve with smoked turkey or chicken. You'll need:

1 pound rhubarb, chopped
1 15-ounce can apricots
1 cup golden raisins
1/4 cup apple cider vinegar

1 cup onion, chopped
1/2 cup sugar
1 teaspoon allspice, ground
1 teaspoon ginger, ground

In a saucepan, put vinegar, 1/3 cup apricot syrup, allspice, and ginger together. Stir over medium heat, cover, and simmer 20 minutes.
Add remaining ingredients. Cook 10-15 more minutes until mixture thickens.

Yield: 2 pints   Serves: 16 (1/8 cup each)   Calories: 40

Fruited Barbecue Sauce

This is truly a summer delight over chicken or ribs.

1-1/2 teaspoon olive oil
1 onion, minced
2 teaspoons garlic, minced
2 cups ketchup
1 tablespoon Worcestershire sauce
1 teaspoon cayenne pepper
2 teaspoons Tabasco™ sauce
2 tablespoons brown sugar
2 tablespoons peach or apricot spread (Sorrel Ridge™)
1 ripe peach, chopped
1 ripe nectarine, chopped

In a large skillet, heat oil over medium heat. Add onion and garlic and sauté 1-2 minutes. Stir in all remaining ingredients. Simmer over low heat 15-20 minutes.

Yield: 3 cups   Serving size: 2 tablespoons   Calories: 40

Hollandaise á l'Orange

1/2 cup orange juice   **2 eggs**
2 tablespoons butter   **Grated peel of 1 orange**
1 teaspoon cornstarch   **1/4 cup milk**

Bring juice to boil for 10 minutes, so that it resembles syrup. Cool.
Melt butter in a pan, remove from heat and add cornstarch. Whisk until smooth (2 minutes). Whisk egg and milk.
Add all ingredients together and cook over low heat until thick. Stir constantly. Serve over veggies.

Serves: 8   Calories: 50

Cranberry Butter for Fish

Top your favorite broiled or grilled fish with this mixture. You'll need:

1/2 cup cranberries, fresh or frozen
3 tablespoons orange juice
1 tablespoon honey
1 teaspoon shallot, minced
1 teaspoon orange zest
2 tablespoons butter, softened (reserve)

In a saucepan, heat all ingredients except butter. Bring to boil, reduce heat and simmer for 2-3 minutes.
Cool mixture and cream butter into it.

Serves: 3   Calories: approx. 232

Vinaigrette

This is an easy and quick dressing.

1 teaspoon garlic, minced
1/2 teaspoon salt
1 teaspoon coarse mustard
Juice of 1 lemon

1/3 cup olive oil
2 teaspoons balsamic vinegar
1/2 teaspoon freshly ground pepper

Whisk all ingredients in a small bowl and serve.

Serving size: 2 tablespoons   Calories: 70 per serving

Apple Barbecue Sauce

This sauce is great on chicken! You'll need the following:

1 cup apples, diced
1/4 cup light brown sugar
2 tablespoons apple cider vinegar
1/4 teaspoon cayenne pepper
1/4 teaspoon ground clover
1/4 cup water

In a 1-quart pot place apples and water together. Boil for 10 minutes on high heat, stirring constantly. Add remaining ingredients; boil 1 minute and reduce heat to low and cook 2 more minutes.

Serves: 6   Calories: 20

DESSERTS

Apple Crisp

Preheat oven to 350°.

Juice of 1 lemon
4 large Granny Smith apples,* sliced into thin chunks
1/2 cup unsweetened apple juice
2 tablespoons maple syrup or brown sugar
1/4 teaspoon lemon zest
3/4 teaspoon cinnamon.

*Granny Smith apples take longer to cook than softer apples like Macintosh.
Mix all the above and place in baking dish sprayed with Pam.

Topping:

1/2 cup rolled oats
3 tablespoons light brown sugar
3 tablespoons whole-wheat flour
2 tablespoons butter
1/4 cup chopped nuts (optional)

Mix topping ingredients until rice size. Sprinkle over apple mixture and bake in preheated oven for 20 to 30 minutes at 350°.

Serves: 9   Calories: 134

Macadamia Nut Cookies

1/2 cup butter, soft
1/2 cup brown sugar
2 tablespoons milk

1-1/2 teaspoon cinnamon
2 cups flour
3/4 cup chopped nuts

Cream butter, sugar, and add the rest of the ingredients. Drop by teaspoonfuls onto cookie sheet. Or make into balls and roll in sugar, more nuts, or oats, and flatten with bottom of glass. Bake at 375° for 7 to 10 minutes.

Yield: 48 cookies   Calories: 52

Chocolate Torte

This recipe satisfies the heart and soul! It has almost no cholesterol and very little sodium. Worth baking? YES! You'll need:

Nonstick cooking spray
1 cup all-purpose flour
2 tablespoons cocoa powder (unsweetened)
1-1/4 teaspoon baking powder
1/4 cup margarine
2/3 cup sugar
3/4 teaspoon vanilla
1/2 cup ice-cold water
2 egg whites

Topping:

1-1/4-ounce envelope whipped dessert topping
2 tablespoons unsweetened cocoa powder
1/2 cup skim milk
1/2 teaspoon vanilla
One 11-ounce can mandarin orange sections (optional)
   (this adds 5 calories per serving)
   OR
2 tablespoons walnuts or pecans (optional)
   (this adds 4 calories per serving)

Preheat oven to 375°. Spray a 9-inch-round pan with cooking spray. In a small bowl, combine flour, 2 tablespoons cocoa powder, and baking powder.

In another bowl beat margarine until creamy, add sugar and 3/4 teaspoon vanilla. Add dry ingredients and cold water, alternating at low speed until smooth. Wash off beaters.

In a clean bowl beat egg whites until peaks form. Fold into batter using a little at a time. Turn into prepared pan and bake at 375° for 20 to 25 minutes. Cool 10 minutes on a wire rack. Remove from pan when cool.

In a small bowl, combine dessert topping mix and 2 tablespoons of cocoa. Add milk and 1/2 teaspoon vanilla and beat at high speed until soft peaks form.

To assemble Torte: Cut the cake horizontally into 2 layers. Place the bottom layer on a plate and top with 1/3 of whipped topping, sprinkle with nuts or oranges (optional). Place top layer on cake and spread the remaining chocolate on top; garnish with nuts or oranges (optional).

Other garnishes:
Coconut — 2 tablespoons (adds 4 calories per serving).
Instant coffee (1 tablespoon can be added to the whipped topping to make Mocha).
Sprinkle wheat germ or bran flakes into the batter.
Cherries (fresh) — 12 adds 5 calories per serving.
Add rum or mint extract in place of vanilla.

Serves: 12   Calories: 152

Indian Pudding

This dessert goes well with a Pot Roast supper (page 82). It is the perfect comfort food for those windy Nantucket evenings. Preheat oven to 325°.

4 cups skim milk or evaporated skim milk
1 tablespoon safflower oil
1 tablespoon margarine
1/2 cup yellow cornmeal
1/2 cup molasses
1/4 cup sugar
1 chopped apple
1/4 cup raisins
4 teaspoons cinnamon
2 egg whites or 1 egg

In a pot, stir 3 cups of milk with oil and margarine over medium heat. Mix 1/2 cup of milk with cornmeal and add to the mixture. Cook for 20 minutes, stirring constantly.

Stir in molasses, sugar, apple, raisins, egg, and spices. Cook another 5 minutes or so until thicker. Pour into a greased 10 x 10-inch baking dish.

Pour remaining 1/2 cup milk on top and bake 1-1/2 hours or until toothpick when inserted comes out clean. Serve warm.

Serves: 10   Calories: 171

Apple Cobbler

6 medium apples, cored, peeled, and chopped
1/4 cup maple syrup
3/4 teaspoon ground cinnamon
1/2 teaspoon nutmeg
1 cup flour/grains (mix 1/2 cup all-purpose flour, 1/4 cup oats, 1/4 cup whole wheat flour)
1 tablespoon sugar
1 teaspoon baking powder
1/4 teaspoon baking soda
3 tablespoons canola oil
1/2 cup buttermilk
1 teaspoon vanilla

Preheat oven to 375°. In a large bowl, combine apples, maple syrup, cinnamon, and nutmeg. Turn into a greased baking dish.

Combine the flours, powder, soda. Set aside. Mix buttermilk, oil, and vanilla. Gradually, add in the flour mixture until moist. Drop in spoonfuls onto apples.

Bake for 40 minutes or until golden-brown.

Serves: 8   Calories: 133

Chocolate (or Vanilla) Custard

This custard is made with egg whites. However, you may use Egg Beaters in place of the egg whites. 4 Egg Beaters = 8 egg whites.

8 egg whites
2 cups chocolate-flavored low-fat milk
  (use 2 cups 1% milk for Vanilla Custard)
1 teaspoon vanilla or brandy flavor
1/4 cup sugar
Boiling water

In a large pan, whisk egg whites. Stir in milk, sugar, and vanilla.

Place six 6-ounce custard cups in a 13 x 9 x 2-inch baking pan on an oven rack. Pour milk mixture into the greased custard cups.

Pour boiling water into the baking pan around the custard cups, one inch deep.

Bake at 325° for 35 minutes. Serve warm or chilled.

You can garnish the custard with Grapenuts, nuts, or wheat germ.

Serves: 6   Calories: approx. 112 each cup

Apricot Tart

This is a great low-fat dessert! You'll need the following:

1/2 pound dried apricots
1/2 jar Sorrell Ridge™ apricot spread
1 frozen puff pastry
1/2 Golden Delicious apple, sliced

Preheat oven to 350°.

On a greased baking pan (13 x 9 inches) roll out puff pastry to meet edges. Prick with a fork.

Spread a thin coat of apricot fruit spread over pastry.

Arrange dried apricots and sliced apples on the dough. Top with remaining fruit spread.

Bake for 25 to 30 minutes; let the top brown.

Serves: 6   Calories: 185

Ginger Snaps

Add chopped nuts to this recipe for a change. You'll need:

1/2 cup brown sugar
1-1/4 cup molasses
3 tablespoons oil (canola), butter, or margarine
2 teaspoons cinnamon
1/2 teaspoon ginger
1/2 teaspoon ground cloves
3-1/2 cups whole-wheat pastry flour*
1 tablespoon baking powder

* For a lighter cookie, use 1-1/2 cups all-purpose flour and 2 cups whole-wheat pastry flour (available at the health-food store)

Heat brown sugar, molasses, and oil until liquid. Add the spices to the molasses mixture. Sift the flour and baking powder and fold into molasses mixture also. Mix into stiff dough.

Drop by tablespoons onto oiled cookie sheet and flatten the cookies with the bottom of a floured glass.

Bake 10 to 12 minutes at 350°.

Yields: Twenty 3-inch cookies   Calories: 95

Strawberry Creme Tart

2 cups milk
1 egg
1/4 cup sugar
1 teaspoon vanilla
1 tablespoon flour
1 pint strawberries
3 tablespoons raspberry fruit spread
2 tablespoons water
Phyllo dough sheets

Preheat the oven to 350°. Spray a cake pan with cooking oil and place three sheets of phyllo dough on top of each other on the pan. Bake until golden, about 5 to 10 minutes.

Meanwhile, in a saucepan, stir milk, sugar, vanilla, egg, and flour over medium heat until thick and bubbly. (To prevent the flour from clumping, you may want to add flour first to 1/2 cup milk and shake before adding it to the pan.)

Pour custard into phyllo. Top with sliced strawberries or other fruit.

In a small saucepan, add fruit spread and water. Stir over medium-high heat until smooth. Pour **slowly** over the strawberries.

Variations: You can use raspberries and blueberries, mixed; or kiwi and strawberries; or bananas and strawberries.

Serves: 6   Calories: approx. 120

Pecan Turtles

1 large chocolate bar (Symphony™)
Pecan halves
Kraft™ caramels

Preheat oven to 350°.
Spray cookie sheet with cooking oil.
Place caramels 1 inch apart on sheet. Warm caramels in oven for about 3 minutes, until softened. (Watch carefully so they don't burn.)
Meanwhile, melt chocolate bar in double boiler on stove.
Take caramels from oven and flatten them. Place about 4 pecan halves on top of each.
Spoon about 1 tablespoon of melted chocolate on top. Let cool and serve.

Calories: about 136 each

Rich Fudge Brownie Torte

1/2 cup or 1 stick butter   **1/2 cup flour**
3 squares unsweetened chocolate   **1/4 teaspoon baking powder**
2 eggs   **1 teaspoon vanilla**
1 cup sugar   **1/2 cup walnuts or pecans, chopped**

In a double boiler melt butter and chocolate. Remove from heat and add remaining ingredients.
Pour into a greased and floured 9-inch pie pan. Bake at 325° for 20 minutes. Serve with ice cream or fresh whipped cream.

Serves: 6   Calories: approx. 327

Rice Pudding

This is a good lower-fat dessert choice. You'll need:

3/4 cups rice (Carolina™)
1/2 gallon milk
2-1/2 tablespoons butter
3 eggs
1 cup sugar
2 teaspoons vanilla

Cook all ingredients over medium heat for about 1 hour. Stir constantly.

Serves: 10   Calories: 192

No-Sugar Cookies

All-natural fruit sugar creates this healthy cookie. Here's what you'll need:

1 cup raisins
1/2 cup well-chopped apples
1/2 cup chopped dates
1 cup water
1/2 cup margarine
1/2 cup each all-purpose and whole-wheat flour
1 teaspoon baking soda
1 teaspoon vanilla
1 cup rolled oats
2 eggs, beaten
3/4 cup nuts, chopped

Boil first 4 ingredients for 3 minutes over low heat. Add margarine mix.
Cool a bit and add remaining ingredients. Mix. Refrigerate overnight or for 4 hours.
Drop by spoonfuls onto greased cookie sheet and bake at 350° for 10 minutes

Yield: 36 cookies   Calories: approx. 40 each

Oat Nut Bars

Although this recipe is higher in fat, it does contain some quality nutrients: peanut butter and oatmeal. You'll need:

2/3 cup butter
1 cup brown sugar
4 cups oatmeal
1/4 cup light corn syrup
3 teaspoons vanilla
1/4 cup flour
1 egg
2/3 cup chunky peanut butter
6 ounces chocolate chunks or chips

In a large bowl, cream butter with sugar and add oatmeal, corn syrup, and vanilla.
Spray a 13 x 9-inch pan with cooking oil and dust it with flour. Put the batter into the pan and bake at 350° for 10 to 15 minutes.
In a double boiler, melt peanut butter with chocolate. Spread over the top of the bars. Cool or refrigerate.

Yield: 24 bars   Calories: 125 per bar

Boston Cream Pie, Nantucket Style

Cake:

6 tablespoons butter, softened
3/4 cup sugar
2 eggs
1/3 cup milk
1 cup flour
1-1/2 teaspoon baking powder
1 teaspoon vanilla extract

Preheat oven to 375°. Grease with cooking spray a 9-inch cake pan.

In a large bowl, beat butter with sugar until smooth. Add eggs, vanilla, and milk and beat again. Beat in flour and baking powder for about 3 minutes at medium speed. Mixture should be pourable.

Pour batter into pan. Bake approximately 25 minutes, or until toothpick inserted in the center comes out clean. Cool in pan.

Cream filling:

2 cups milk
1/4 cup sugar
1 egg
1 teaspoon vanilla
2 tablespoons flour or cornstarch

Set aside 1/4 cup milk in a shaker jar (jar with a lid). Add remaining milk, sugar, eggs, and vanilla to a 2-quart saucepan set on medium-low heat. Shake flour with reserved milk and add to pan. Stir constantly until mixture boils and thickens, approximately 20 minutes. Remove from heat and set aside to cool.

Chocolate icing:

1/4 stick of butter, soft
2 tablespoons cocoa powder
1-1/2 to 2 cups confectioner's sugar
1 teaspoon instant coffee diluted in 1 tablespoon warm water (optional)
Milk

Beat butter; add cocoa and sugar. Add milk to attain desired consistency.

Putting it all together: Remove cooled cake from pan. Cut the cake in half, horizontally. Spread bottom layer with cooled custard. Place top layer on and ice with chocolate icing.

Refrigerate until ready to use.

Serves: 8   Calories: 236

Orange Souffle´

It's nice to dress up this elegant dessert with raspberry sauce. For the souffle´ you'll need:

4 tablespoons butter
1/3 cup flour
1/8 teaspoon salt
1-1/2 cup milk
3 tablespoons sugar

4 egg yolks
1/3 cup orange-flavor liqueur
1 tablespoon grated orange rind
6 egg whites, room temperature
1/4 teaspoon cream of tartar

Preheat oven to 375°.

In a saucepan over low heat, melt butter. Stir in flour and salt. Slowly add milk and stir until thickened. Remove from heat.

With a wire whisk, beat 3 tablespoons of sugar into mixture. Quickly beat in egg yolks until well mixed. Stir in orange peel and liqueur. Set aside.

Spray souffle´ dish or baking dish with cooking oil. Sprinkle with sugar if desired.

In a large bowl, beat egg whites and cream of tartar until stiff peaks form. Fold in mixture with a whisk or spatula.

Pour mixture in souffle´ dish. With the back of a spoon make a 1-inch indentation around edge of dish. This makes the souffle´ rise high.

Bake 30 -35 minutes at 375°.

Serves: 6   Calories: 155

Impossible Pie

For this delicious and easy dessert you'll need:

4 eggs
1/4 cup margarine or butter
1 cup sugar
1/2 cup flour
1/4 teaspoon salt

2 cups milk
1 teaspoon vanilla
1 cup coconut
1/2 teaspoon baking powder

Place all ingredients in blender at one time and mix together. Pour into a buttered 10-inch pie plate.

Bake for 1 hour at 350´.

When done, crust will be on bottom, custard in the middle, coconut on top.

Servings: 8   Calories: 258

Maple Fudge

To be indulgent every once in a while...this recipe is not bad in fat (3 grams per serving).

2 cups maple syrup
2 cups maple sugar or granulated sugar
1/2 cup half-and-half
1/4 cup light corn syrup
2 tablespoons sweet butter
1 cup walnuts, chopped
2 squares unsweetened chocolate, melted

Prepare an 8 x 8 pan by spraying with cooking oil.

In a heavy 3-quart saucepan, combine maple syrup, sugar, half-and-half, and corn syrup. Heat over medium heat and bring to a boil, stirring until ingredients combine.

Cook, **without** stirring, until mixture reaches 236° on a candy thermometer (or until some of mixture forms a ball when dropped in cold water).

Remove from heat, stir in butter. Beat by hand or with an electric mixer until thickened.

Fold in nuts and melted chocolate. Pour into pan.

Cool to room temperature.

Yield: 36 squares   Calories: 125

Grilled Fruit

Serve this favorite recipe with chilled custard (page 152), yogurt, or ice cream.
The ingredients are:

2 red apples (Red Delicious)
2 green apples (Granny Smith)
2 pears (Bosc or Bartlett)
1/4 cup brandy or 1 tablespoon brandy flavoring
1 tablespoon lemon juice
1 tablespoon lemon peel
1 tablespoon honey or maple sugar

Heat coals on grill. Place grill rack 4-5 inches above coals.

Remove all stems from fruit. Cut each into six sections.

In a small bowl, mix remaining ingredients.

Alternate fruit on metal skewers. Brush with mixture and grill for 30 minutes, turning frequently.

Serves: 8   Calories: 55 per serving with custard

Lemon Meringue Bars

This is an easy alternative to the pie. You'll need:

1 cup flour (for crust)
3 tablespoons butter
1/4 cup sugar (for crust)
4 eggs
1 cup sugar (for top)

Grated rind of 1 lemon
Juice of 1 lemon
1 tablespoon flour (for top)
2 egg whites
3 tablespoons sugar (for meringue)

Preheat oven to 350°.

Crust:

Blend 1/4 cup sugar, 1 egg, butter, and 1 cup flour in a bowl. Add a little water if needed. Pat dough evenly into a greased 13 x 9 pan.
Bake at 350° for 10 minutes.

Top:

Beat remaining 3 eggs and 1 cup sugar until fluffy. Add lemon rind, lemon juice, and 1 table-spoon flour. Mix and pour over crust.
Bake at 350° for 15 minutes.

Meringue:

Beat egg whites until frothy. Add 3 tablespoons sugar and continue beating until stiff peaks form.
Spread over lemon bars.
Raise oven temperature to 450° and bake 5 more minutes.
Cool; cut with wet knife.

Yield: 20   Calories: 78

German Chocolate Cake

Bake a traditional dark chocolate cake, 8 to 9 inches round. Cool and fill with coconut filling, for which you'll need:

Filling:

1 cup evaporated milk
1 cup sugar, granulated
1-2 egg yolks
1/2 cup butter (1 stick)

1 teaspoon vanilla
1-1/3 cup flaked coconut
1 cup chopped pecans

In a saucepan, mix milk, sugar, egg yolks, butter, and vanilla. Cook and stir over medium heat until mixture thickens (about 10 minutes).

Remove from heat, add coconut and pecans. Cool until mixture spreads easily. Use this for center filling and top of cake.

Frosting:

1/2 stick butter
1 to 1-1/2 cup confectioner's sugar
3 tablespoons cocoa powder
1 teaspoon strong coffee (cooled)

In a bowl beat butter, add remaining ingredients, and beat until smooth. Add either more sugar or coffee to make it smooth.

Use this frosting for side and decoration of cake. Refrigerate.

Serves: 8   Calories: approx. 560

Pecan Bars

Great frozen! Watch it, these are addicting. For this dessert you'll need the following ingredients:

Base:

1/2 package yellow cake mix
1/3 cup butter, softened
Flour

Filling:

14-ounce can sweetened condensed milk
1 egg
1 teaspoon vanilla
1 cup chopped pecans

Heat oven to 350°. Grease 13 x 9-inch pan.
Combine base; press it into pan. If too moist, sprinkle a bit of flour into it.
In a bowl, beat first three ingredients of filling. Stir in pecans. Pour evenly over base.
Bake at 350° until light brown in color, about 25 to 35 minutes.
Cool completely.
Variations: Add one egg to base or use walnuts and chocolate chips.

Servings: 8   Calories: 320

Cheesecake

Crust:

1-1/2 cup Graham cracker crumbs
3 tablespoons sugar (optional)
1 teaspoon cinnamon (optional)
1/2 cup melted butter

Mix together; place in pan and press up into side.

Filling:

8 ounces Ricotta cheese
Two 8-ounce packages cream cheese, softened
1/2 cup sugar
1 teaspoon grated lemon peel
1 tablespoon lemon juice
1 teaspoon vanilla
2 eggs, separated

In large bowl, beat cheese until fluffy.
Add sugar, lemon peel, juice, and vanilla; beat, then add egg yolks.
Beat egg whites until stiff and fold into the mixture.
Bake at 300° for 55 minutes.
Variations: Add fruit filling at the bottom of crust.

Servings: 8-10   Calories: approx. 400

Tunnel of Fudge Cake

For this luscious chocolate dessert, you'll need:

1-1/2 cup butter, softened
1-1/2 cup sugar
6 eggs
2 cups flour
1 package (regular size) Double Dutch Fudge Frosting Mix
2 cups chopped walnuts

Preheat oven to 350°.
In large bowl, cream butter and add eggs, one at a time. Beat well after adding each egg.
Gradually add sugar; continue creaming until light and fluffy.
No need to sift flour — measure by lightly spooning into cup. By hand, stir in flour, dry frosting mix, and walnuts until well blended.
Pour batter into greased 10-inch Bundt pan. Bake at 350° for 60 to 65 minutes.
Cool for two hours before removing from pan.

Serves: 10   Calories: 429

Carrot Cake

This cake can be made in form pans, such as bunnies or lambs, and used as a centerpiece for Passover or Easter dinner. Just sprinkle shredded coconut on top. You'll need the following ingredients:

2 cups sugar
2 teaspoons cinnamon
2 to 3 cups grated carrots
4 eggs
2 cups self-rising flour
1/2 teaspoon each baking soda and baking powder
2 sticks butter, melted

In a large bowl beat eggs; add sugar, then butter. Cream together.
Add remaining ingredients; mix well.
Pour into two 9-inch round pans.
Bake at 350° for 40 minutes or until toothpick inserted comes out clean. Cool.

Icing:

1 package (8 ounces) cream cheese, soft
1 stick butter
1 teaspoon vanilla
1 box confectioner's sugar

In a bowl, mix cream cheese and butter. Add sugar and vanilla; mix until smooth. Ice cake only after it has cooled.

Variations: Add food coloring to icing and decorate with flower patterns.

Servings: 10   Calories: 449

Krumkake

These Norwegian Cone Cookies are a tradition with my family during the holidays. You can fill them with berries, ice cream, or other goodies. Plain, they are especially delicate cookies to serve with tea.

3 eggs   **1/2 cup flour**
1/2 cup sugar   **1 teaspoon vanilla or almond extract**
1/2 cup margarine

In a medium bowl, beat eggs and sugar for about 3 minutes.
Melt margarine, cool it slightly, then add it to the mixture.
Add flour and extract; stir until smooth.
Heat the Krumkake or pizzelle ungreased iron. Place about 1 tablespoon of the cookie mixture in the middle of the preheated iron. Close gently but firmly for about 30 seconds. Open iron carefully, loosen cookie, and roll immediately.

Servings: Makes about 25-30 cookies, 62 calories each.

Chocolate Chip Cookies

1 stick butter
3/4 cup brown sugar
1 egg
1 teaspoon vanilla
1 cup flour
1/2 cup oatmeal
1/2 to 1 cup semisweet chocolate chips
1/2 cup chopped walnuts or pecans

Preheat oven to 375°.

In a medium bowl cream butter, add sugar, vanilla, and egg, and mix well.

Add remaining ingredients.

On a greased cookie sheet, place rounded tablespoons of dough spaced evenly about 2 inches apart. Bake approximately 10 to 12 minutes.

Variations: Add raisins and peanuts and omit oatmeal for a different combination (similar to a Chunky bar). You can also add wheat germ along with the oatmeal or even bran flakes for a cookie with more fiber.

Approx.   20 cookies   Calories: about 120 per cookie